INTRODUCING ISSUES WITH OPPOSING VIEWPOINTS®

Animal Rights

Lauri S. Friedman, *Book Editor*

GREENHAVEN PRESS
A part of Gale, Cengage Learning

GALE
CENGAGE Learning™

Detroit • New York • San Francisco • New Haven, Conn • Waterville, Maine • London

Christine Nasso, *Publisher*
Elizabeth Des Chenes, *Managing Editor*

© 2011 Greenhaven Press, a part of Gale, Cengage Learning

LIBRARY OF CONGRESS CATALOGING-IN-PUBLICATION DATA
Animal rights / Lauri S. Friedman, book editor.
p. cm. -- (Introducing issues with opposing viewpoints)
Includes bibliographical references and index.
ISBN 978-0-7377-4937-3 (hbk.)
1. Animal rights--Juvenile literature. I. Friedman, Lauri S.
HV4708.A5494 2010
179'.3--dc22
2010023000

Printed in the United States of America
1 2 3 4 5 6 7 14 13 12 11 10

Contents

Foreword

I ndulging in a wide spectrum of ideas, beliefs, and perspectives is a critical cornerstone of democracy. After all, it is often debates over differences of opinion, such as whether to legalize abortion, how to treat prisoners, or when to enact the death penalty, that shape our society and drive it forward. Such diversity of thought is frequently regarded as the hallmark of a healthy and civilized culture. As the Reverend Clifford Schutjer of the First Congregational Church in Mansfield, Ohio, declared in a 2001 sermon, "Surrounding oneself with only like-minded people, restricting what we listen to or read only to what we find agreeable is irresponsible. Refusing to entertain doubts once we make up our minds is a subtle but deadly form of arrogance." With this advice in mind, Introducing Issues with Opposing Viewpoints books aim to open readers' minds to the critically divergent views that comprise our world's most important debates.

Introducing Issues with Opposing Viewpoints simplifies for students the enormous and often overwhelming mass of material now available via print and electronic media. Collected in every volume is an array of opinions that captures the essence of a particular controversy or topic. Introducing Issues with Opposing Viewpoints books embody the spirit of nineteenth-century journalist Charles A. Dana's axiom: "Fight for your opinions, but do not believe that they contain the whole truth, or the only truth." Absorbing such contrasting opinions teaches students to analyze the strength of an argument and compare it to its opposition. From this process readers can inform and strengthen their own opinions, or be exposed to new information that will change their minds. Introducing Issues with Opposing Viewpoints is a mosaic of different voices. The authors are statesmen, pundits, academics, journalists, corporations, and ordinary people who have felt compelled to share their experiences and ideas in a public forum. Their words have been collected from newspapers, journals, books, speeches, interviews, and the Internet, the fastest growing body of opinionated material in the world.

Introducing Issues with Opposing Viewpoints shares many of the well-known features of its critically acclaimed parent series, Opposing Viewpoints. The articles are presented in a pro/con format, allowing readers to absorb divergent perspectives side by side. Active reading questions preface each viewpoint, requiring the student to approach the material thoughtfully and carefully. Useful charts, graphs, and cartoons supplement each article. A thorough introduction provides readers with crucial background on an issue. An annotated bibliography points the reader toward articles, books, and Web sites that contain additional information on the topic. An appendix of organizations to contact contains a wide variety of charities, nonprofit organizations, political groups, and private enterprises that each hold a position on the issue at hand. Finally, a comprehensive index allows readers to locate content quickly and efficiently.

Introducing Issues with Opposing Viewpoints is also significantly different from Opposing Viewpoints. As the series title implies, its presentation will help introduce students to the concept of opposing viewpoints, and learn to use this material to aid in critical writing and debate. The series' four-color, accessible format makes the books attractive and inviting to readers of all levels. In addition, each viewpoint has been carefully edited to maximize a reader's understanding of the content. Short but thorough viewpoints capture the essence of an argument. A substantial, thought-provoking essay question placed at the end of each viewpoint asks the student to further investigate the issues raised in the viewpoint, compare and contrast two authors' arguments, or consider how one might go about forming an opinion on the topic at hand. Each viewpoint contains sidebars that include at-a-glance information and handy statistics. A Facts About section located in the back of the book further supplies students with relevant facts and figures.

Following in the tradition of the Opposing Viewpoints series, Greenhaven Press continues to provide readers with invaluable exposure to the controversial issues that shape our world. As John Stuart Mill once wrote: "The only way in which a human being can make some approach to knowing the whole of a subject is by hearing what can be said about it by persons of every variety of opinion and studying all modes in which it can be looked at by every character of mind. No wise man ever acquired his wisdom in any mode but this." It is to this principle that Introducing Issues with Opposing Viewpoints books are dedicated.

Introduction

In the United States, animals are very much a part of human society. Recent years have seen pet ownership skyrocket—The American Society for the Prevention of Cruelty to Animals (ASPCA) estimates that about 63 percent of all households in the United States have a pet, and that there are about 75 million dogs and about 85 million cats in American homes. In upscale neighborhoods of trendy cities, dogs and cats enjoy their own bed and breakfasts, salons, fashion boutiques, and gourmet food lines. Animals even feature as the stars of television shows and movies—for example, 2008's *Marley and Me*, based on the best-selling book, grossed over $143 million and was number one at the box office its opening weekend. Clearly, Americans love their animals. But loving animals is different from supporting their right to life, liberty, and happiness. Thus Americans—even pet owners and animal lovers—continue to disagree on the extent to which animals should be granted rights.

The issues surrounding animal rights are vast, and include whether they should be treated as property, food, entertainment, and used in research. At the heart of all these issues is the question of whether granting animals rights threatens the uniqueness of humans. Some believe that granting animals rights complements the human experience, and is actually an important—even necessary—component of an ethical human existence. Professor Josephine Donovan is one person who believes humans are enhanced by the experience of treating animals compassionately and humanely. "It behooves us as ethical beings to incorporate their wishes when we make decisions," says Donovan.[1]

In fact, animal rights activists such as Donovan argue that encouraging people to treat animals humanely and respectfully will result in a kinder, more equitable society for humans, too. Just as eradicating the pain, suffering, and injustice of other humans leads to a more just and equitable world, so too, argue animal rights activists, does eliminating the pain and suffering of animals contribute to a better society. "Basically, it boils down to cold logic," says author Richard Ryder. "If we are going to care about the suffering of other humans then logically we should care about the suffering of non-humans too."[2] This was one of the rationales behind Spain's 2008 push to grant Great Apes legal personhood. According to philosopher Paula Casal, executive director of the Great Ape Project, which has advocated for the Spanish initiative, Spain's interest in granting rights to apes evolved out of the March 2004 terrorist attacks in Madrid that killed 192 people. "The Madrid bombing made many people think about the consequences of selfishly letting one's compatriots act wrongly,"[3] said Casal. In other words, if society wanted to eliminate the factors that had contributed to terrorism—the ultimate disrespect for life—it needed to start by encouraging widespread respect for all life, even that which is not human.

Yet the suggestion that apes be made legally on par with humans was met with opposition and even outright anger by many. Some argued that assigning human rights to animals is nothing less than a denial of what it means to be human, an endeavor that could actually diminish human rights. Margaret Somerville, director of the Centre for Medicine, Ethics and Law at McGill University, is one person who believes that granting animals human-like rights threatens not only the uniqueness of humans but the quality of the rights they currently enjoy. "If animals

An orangutan holds her baby at the Barcelona Zoo. In 2008, Spain passed legislation that, if approved, would grant apes legal personhood.

become persons," writes Somerville, "human persons become animals. The line between humans and other animals is blurred and the idea that humans are 'special' and deserve 'special respect' is eliminated."[4] For Somerville, this is not just an egotistical distinction. She points out that if humans and animals are to be regarded as interchangeable, then "that means that what we do or don't do to 'animal persons' should be the same as what we do or don't do to 'human persons.' So, for instance, if we have euthanasia for animals, we should, likewise, have it for humans. If we don't eat humans, we shouldn't eat animals."[5] In other words, treating animals like humans, and vice versa, threatens to fundamentally reduce the quality and character of the human experience.

Still other animal rights opponents argue it is inappropriate to expend energy securing rights for animals when so many humans have yet to fully enjoy rights. According to the organization Freedom House, which ranks each of the world's 193 countries and 16 territories as either "not free," "partly free," or "free," in 2009, 62 countries were ranked as only "partly free," and 42 were ranked as "not free." Together, that is 104 countries— or 54 percent, the majority—whose citizens do not yet enjoy all of the rights and freedoms they should. Given this stark reality, animal rights opponents argue that efforts to attain rights should remain focused on human beneficiaries before attempting to secure them for other species.

Whether granting animals rights threatens or enhances the human experience is one of the many arguments presented in *Introducing Issues with Opposing Viewpoints: Animal Rights*. Pro/con article pairs also explore whether animals should be treated as property; eaten as food; used in the manufacturing of products; and involved in both medical and commercial research. The guided reading questions and essay prompts encourage readers to develop their own opinions on this timelessly controversial topic.

Notes

1. Josephine Donovan, "Caring for Animals: a Feminist Approach," *Tikkun*, January–February, 2009. www.tikkun.org/article.php/jan09 _donovan.
2. Richard Ryder, "All Beings That Feel Pain Deserve Human Rights," *Guardian* (Manchester), August 6, 2005. www.guardian.co.uk.2005/ aug/06/animalwelfare.

3. Quoted in Hugh Warwick, "Moral Booster," *Guardian* (Manchester), June 7, 2006. http://www.guardian.co.uk/society/2006/jun/07/guardiansocietysupplement3.

4. Margaret Somerville, "Dolphins and Chimpanzees Should Be Respected, but They Are Not Persons," MercatorNet, January 27, 2010. http://www.mercatornet.com/articles/view/are_animals_ persons/.

5. Margaret Somerville, "Dolphins and Chimpanzees Should Be Respected, but They Are Not Persons."

Chapter 1

Should Animals Have Rights?

A group from the Massachusetts Animal Rights Coalition protests against the use of horse-drawn carriages in Boston. They argue that the horses are exploited and abused.

Viewpoint

1

Animals Deserve Rights Similar to Humans

Richard Ryder

> *"If we are going to care about the suffering of other humans then logically we should care about the suffering of non-humans too."*

In the following viewpoint Richard Ryder explains why he believes animals deserve rights similar to humans. Ryder says that humans evolved from animals and share many characteristics with them. In particular, both humans and animals are capable of feeling pain and suffering. As such, Ryder believes they should never inflict pain and suffering on each other. He believes that harming animals cuts humans off from their origins and from the animalistic parts of themselves. Because of the human-animal link, Ryder believes it is immoral to abuse animals or cause them suffering. He concludes that animals deserve to be legally protected from pain and suffering the same way humans are.

Ryder is the author of *Painism: A Modern Morality* and *Putting Morality Back into Politics*.

AS YOU READ, CONSIDER THE FOLLOWING QUESTIONS:
1. What relates humans to all other animals, in Ryder's opinion?
2. What does the word "painient" mean in the context of the view-point?
3. According to the author, what is worse than inflicting a single unit of pain on a thousand individuals? How does this relate to his argument?

The word speciesism came to me while I was lying in a bath in Oxford some 35 years ago. It was like racism or sexism—a prejudice based upon morally irrelevant physical differences.

We Are All Animals, and We All Feel Pain

Since Darwin we have known we are human animals related to all the other animals through evolution; how, then, can we justify our almost total oppression of all the other species? All animal species can suffer pain and distress. Animals scream and writhe like us; their nervous systems are similar and contain the same biochemicals that we know are associated with the experience of pain in ourselves.

Our concern for the pain and distress of others should be extended to any "painient"—pain-feeling—being regardless of his or her sex, class, race, religion, nationality or species. Indeed, if aliens from outer space turn out to be painient, or if we ever manufacture machines who are painient, then we must widen the moral circle to include them. Painience is the only convincing basis for attributing rights or, indeed, interests to others.

Many other qualities, such as "inherent value", have been suggested. But value cannot exist in the absence of consciousness or potential consciousness. Thus, rocks and rivers and houses have no interests and no rights of their own. This does not mean, of course, that they are not of value to us, and to many other painients, including those who need them as habitats and who would suffer without them.

The Banishment of Suffering

Many moral principles and ideals have been proposed over the centuries—justice, freedom, equality, brotherhood, for example. But these are mere stepping stones to the ultimate good, which is happiness; and happiness is made easier by freedom from all forms of pain and suffering (using the words "pain" and "suffering" interchangeably). Indeed, if you think about it carefully you can see that the reason why these other ideals are considered important is that people have believed that they are essential to the banishment of suffering. In fact they do sometimes have this result, but not always.

Why emphasise pain and other forms of suffering rather than pleasure and happiness? One answer is that pain is much more powerful than

Animal rights activists argue that caring for animals enhances the human experience.

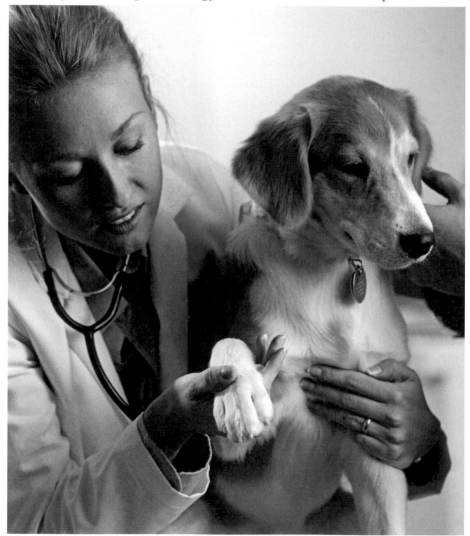

pleasure. Would you not rather avoid an hour's torture than gain an hour's bliss? Pain is the one and only true evil. What, then, about the masochist? The answer is that pain gives him pleasure that is greater than his pain!

Inflicting Any Kind of Pain Is Wrong

One of the important tenets of painism (the name I give to my moral approach) is that we should concentrate upon the individual because it is the individual—not the race, the nation or the species—who does the actual suffering. For this reason, the pains and pleasures of several individuals cannot meaningfully be aggregated, as occurs in utilitarianism and most moral theories. One of the problems with the utilitarian view is that, for example, the sufferings of a gang-rape victim can be justified if the rape gives a greater sum total of pleasure to the rapists. But consciousness, surely, is bounded by the boundaries of the individual. My pain and the pain of others are thus in separate categories; you cannot add or subtract them from each other. They are worlds apart.

Without directly experiencing pains and pleasures they are not really there—we are counting merely their husks. Thus, for example, inflicting 100 units of pain on one individual is, I would argue, far worse than inflicting a single unit of pain on a thousand or a million individuals, even though the total of pain in the latter case is far greater. In any situation we should thus concern ourselves primarily with the pain of the individual who is the maximum sufferer. It does not matter, morally speaking, who or what the maximum sufferer is—whether human, non-human or machine. Pain is pain regardless of its host.

Suffering Must Be Treated Equally
Across Different Species

Of course, each species is different in its needs and in its reactions. What is painful for some is not necessarily so for others. So we can treat different species differently, but we should always treat equal suffering equally. In the case of non-humans, we see them mercilessly exploited in factory farms, in laboratories and in the wild. A whale may take 20 minutes to die after being harpooned. A lynx may suffer for a week with her broken leg held in a steel-toothed trap. A battery hen lives all her life unable to even stretch her wings. An animal in a toxicity test, poisoned with a household product, may linger in agony for hours or days before dying.

These are major abuses causing great suffering. Yet they are still justified on the grounds that these painients are not of the same species as ourselves. It is almost as if some people had not heard of Darwin! We treat the other animals not as relatives but as unfeeling things. We would not dream of treating our babies, or mentally handicapped adults, in these ways—yet these humans are sometimes less intelligent and less able to communicate with us than are some exploited non-humans.

The Logic of Kindness

The simple truth is that we exploit the other animals and cause them suffering because we are more powerful than they are. Does this mean that if those aforementioned aliens landed on Earth and turned out to be far more powerful than us we would let them—without argument—chase and kill us for sport, experiment on us or breed us in factory farms, and turn us into tasty humanburgers? Would we accept their explanation that it was perfectly moral for them to do all these things as we were not of their species?

Basically, it boils down to cold logic. If we are going to care about the suffering of other humans then logically we should care about the suffering of non-humans too. It is the heartless exploiter of animals, not the animal protectionist, who is being irrational, showing a sentimental tendency to put his own species on a pedestal. We all, thank goodness, feel a natural spark of sympathy for the sufferings of others. We need to catch that spark and fan it into a fire of rational and universal compassion.

Laws Are Needed to Protect the Rights of Animals

All of this has implications, of course. If we gradually bring non-humans into the same moral and legal circle as ourselves then we will not be able to exploit them as our slaves. Much progress has been made with sensible new European legislation in recent decades, but there is still a very long way to go. Some international recognition of the moral status of animals is long overdue. There are various conservation treaties, but nothing at UN [United Nations] level, for example, that recognises the rights, interests or welfare of the animals themselves. That must, and I believe will, change.

EVALUATING THE AUTHOR'S ARGUMENTS:

Ryder offers several examples of when the mistreatment of animals qualifies as "major abuses" that cause "great suffering." List at least three of these examples and state whether or not you agree with Ryder. Do these examples constitute major abuses or are they justifiable? Explain your reasoning.

Animals Do Not Deserve Rights Similar to Humans

William Saletan

> "Opening your mind to science-based animal rights doesn't eliminate inequality. It just makes the inequality more scientific."

In the following viewpoint, William Saletan argues it is inappropriate to grant animals the same rights as humans. Saletan agrees that some animals, like apes, exhibit remarkable qualities and skills. But Saletan argues that not only is an ape fundamentally different from a human, but so too are different species of animals different from each other. A dog, for example, has different capabilities than an ape, which has different qualities than an ant. Therefore, Saletan argues it is inappropriate to treat all animals as equal, since there is no need to give an ant—an emotionally limited creature—the same consideration as an ape, which has many more mental faculties. Drawing such distinctions between animals only proves to Saletan that animals—including humans—are not equal to each other. And if they are not equal, he reasons they do not deserve the same rights. As a

William Saletan, "Animal-Rights Farm: Ape Rights and the Myth of Animal Equality," *Slate*, July 1, 2008. Copyright © 2008 Washingtonpost.Newsweek Interactive. All Rights Reserved. Reproduced by permission.

result, he concludes it is inappropriate to grant animals the same rights as humans.

Saletan is the national correspondent at *Slate*, an online magazine of news, politics, and culture.

AS YOU READ, CONSIDER THE FOLLOWING QUESTIONS:
1. What is the Great Ape Project, and what is their mission, according to Saletan?
2. What does the phrase "a rat, is a pig, is a dog, is a boy" mean in the context of the viewpoint? What is your opinion of this phrase?
3. What does the author say are "appeals to discrimination"? How does this support his argument?

S hould apes be treated like people?

Under a resolution headed for passage in the Spanish parliament, respecting the personal rights of "our non-human brothers" won't just be a good idea. It'll be the law.

Giving Apes Human Protections

The resolution, approved last week [in 2008] by a parliamentary committee with broad support, urges the government to implement the agenda of the Great Ape Project [GAP], an organization whose founding declaration says apes "may not be killed" or "arbitrarily deprived of their liberty." No more routine confinement. According to [news provider] Reuters, the proposal would commit the government to ending involuntary use of apes in circuses, TV ads, and dangerous experiments.

Proponents hail the resolution as the first crack in the "species barrier." Peter Singer, the philosopher who co-founded GAP, puts it this way: "There is no sound moral reason why possession of basic rights should be limited to members of a particular species." If aliens or monkeys are shown to have moral or intellectual abilities similar to ours, we should treat them like people.

He's right. To borrow Martin Luther King's rule, you should be judged by what's inside you, not by what's on the surface.

This chimpanzee at the Madrid Zoo was given legal protection by Spain's legislature in June 2008.

Evolution Made Humans Different from Animals

If the idea of treating chimps like people freaks you out, join the club. Creationists have been fighting this battle for a long time. They realized long ago that evolution threatened humanity's special status.

Maybe you thought all this evolution stuff was just about the past. Surprise! Once you've admitted chimps are your relatives, you have to think about treating them that way. That's why, when the Spanish proposal won approval last week, GAP's leader in Spain called it a victory for "our evolutionary comrades."

Opponents view the resolution as egalitarian extremism. Spain's conservative party frets that it would grant animals the same rights as people. Spanish newspapers and citizens complain that ape rights are distracting lawmakers from human problems. Wesley Smith, my favorite anti-animal-rights blogger, sees the resolution as the first step in a campaign to "elevate all mammals to moral equality with humans." Ultimately, Smith warns, "Animal rights activists believe a rat, is a pig, is a dog, is a boy."

Treating Apes Like Children or the Mentally Incompetent

You can certainly find that theme in some quarters. GAP calls humans, chimps, bonobos, gorillas, and orangutans "members of the community of equals," and Singer holds out the possibility that GAP "may pave the way for the extension of rights to all primates, or all mammals, or all animals." But the arguments GAP has deployed in Spain don't advance the idea of equality among animals. They destroy it.

GAP is scientifically honest. And science doesn't show mental parity between great apes and human adults. What it shows, as the group's president acknowledges, is that great apes "experience an emotional and intellectual conscience similar to that of human children." Accordingly, the Spanish proposal doesn't treat apes like you or me. It treats them like "humans of limited capacity, such as children or those who are mentally incompetent and are afforded guardians or caretakers to represent their interests."

And that's just the top rung of the inequality ladder. GAP's mission statement says great apes are entitled to rights based on their "morally significant characteristics." It says they enjoy a rich emotional and cultural existence in which they experience emotions such as fear, anxiety and happiness. They share the intellectual capacity to create and use tools, learn and teach other languages. They remember their past and plan for their future. It is in recognition of these and other morally significant qualities that the Great Ape Project was founded.

Animals Are Not Equal to Each Other

Morally significant qualities. Morally significant characteristics. These are appeals to discrimination, not universal equality. Most animals don't have a rich cultural life. They can't make tools. They don't teach languages. Singer even points out that "chimpanzees, bonobos and gorillas have long-term relationships, not only between mothers and children, but also between unrelated apes." Special rights for animals in committed relationships! It sounds like a Moral Majority for vegans.

Humans Are "More Equal than Others"

Opening your mind to science-based animal rights doesn't eliminate inequality. It just makes the inequality more scientific. A rat can't match a pig, much less a boy. In fact, as a GAP board member points out, "We are closer genetically to a chimp than a mouse is to a rat."

George Orwell wrote the cruel finale to this tale 63 years ago in *Animal Farm*: "All animals are equal. But some animals are more equal than others." That wasn't how the egalitarian uprising in the book was supposed to turn out. It wasn't how the animal rights movement was supposed to turn out, either.

EVALUATING THE AUTHORS' ARGUMENTS:

Saletan argues that evolution has rendered all animals—including humans—fundamentally different from each other, and as such they do not deserve similar rights. How do you think Richard Ryder, author of the previous viewpoint, would respond to this claim? After reading both viewpoints, with which author do you agree? Why?

Viewpoint

3

Animals Should Be Treated as the Property of Humans

Wesley J. Smith

"[Granting] animal standing . . . would both undermine the status of animals as property and elevate them with the force of law toward legal personhood."

Animals should be viewed as human property and not as individual rights holders argues Wesley J. Smith in the following viewpoint. Smith discusses attempts to allow animals and pets to sue farmers, corporations, and even their owners for mistreatment, imprisonment, and other crimes. Smith warns that giving animals the ability to sue humans elevates them to personhood, a status which they—as animals—do not deserve. Furthermore, allowing animals to sue humans would unfairly cripple businesses that trade in animal products or involve the use of animals. For all of these reasons, Smith concludes it is wiser to regard animals as human property rather than as autonomous individuals with rights.

Smith is a senior fellow in human rights and bioethics at the Discovery Institute. He is also the author of *A Rat Is a Pig Is a Dog Is a Boy: The Human Cost of Animal Rights*.

AS YOU READ, CONSIDER THE FOLLOWING QUESTIONS:
1. What does Smith mean when he says that granting animal rights would allow animal rights activists to attack animal industries "from within"?
2. Who described animals as "voiceless rights-holders"?
3. What is the Cetacean Community, and how does it factor into the author's argument?

I magine you are a cattle rancher looking for liability insurance. You meet with your broker, who, as expected, asks a series of questions to gauge your suitability for coverage:

Have you ever been sued by your cattle?

If the answer is yes, what was the outcome of that suit?

Have you received any correspondence or other communication from your herd's legal representatives threatening suit or seeking to redress any legal grievance?

If you think that's a ridiculous scenario, that animals suing their owners could never happen, think again. For years, the animal rights movement has quietly agitated to enact laws, convince the government to promulgate regulations, or obtain a court ruling granting animals the "legal standing" to drag their owners (and others) into court.

What If Animals Had the Right to Sue Humans?

Animals are not (yet) legal persons or rights-bearing beings, hence, they lack standing to go to court to seek legal redress. That procedural impediment prevents animal rights activists from attacking animal industries "from within," as, for example, by representing lab rats in class action lawsuits against research labs. This lack of legal standing forces attorneys in the burgeoning field of animal law—who are dedicated to impeding, and eventually destroying, all animal industries—to find other legal pretexts by which to bring their targets directly into court.

In 2006, the Humane Society of the United States—which has no affiliation with local humane societies—brought a lawsuit against

Hudson Valley Foie Gras contending the company permitted bird feces to pollute the Hudson River. The Humane Society of the United States isn't an environmental group, so why were they suing about pollution? The answer is that the animal rights group considers its legal adversary to be a "notorious factory farm." But because it had no standing to bring a private case against Hudson Valley as guardians for the farm's ducks, but still wanting to impede the farm's operation, the Humane Society availed itself of the private right to sue directly as permitted under the Clean Water Act.

But imagine if the farm's ducks could sue the farm. The Humane Society or any other animal rights group—who, after all, would be the true litigants—could sue the company into oblivion. Indeed, if animals were granted legal standing, the harm that animal rights activists could do to labs, restaurant chains, mink farms, dog breeders, animal parks, race tracks, etc., would be worse than the destruction wrought by tort lawsuits against the tobacco industry. No wonder animal rights activists salivate at the prospect of animals being allowed to sue.

Animals Have Friends in Powerful Places

Animal standing has friends in some surprisingly high places—including potentially at the highest levels of the Obama administration. Senator Saxby Chambliss of Georgia, ranking Republican member of the Senate Agriculture Committee, recently announced he was hold-

Ducks sit in a force-feeding machine at Hudson Valley Foie Gras. Cities like Chicago have banned the sale of foie gras because of such production methods.

ing up the confirmation of law professor Cass Sunstein—a close friend of the president rumored to be on the fast track for the Supreme Court—as the White House's "regulations czar." The reason: Sunstein explicitly advocates animals' being granted legal standing.

In a 2004 book which he edited, *Animal Rights: Current Debates and New Directions*, Sunstein wrote:

> It seems possible . . . that before long, Congress will grant standing to animals to protect their own rights and interests. . . . Congress might grant standing to animals in their own right, partly to increase the number of private monitors of illegality, and partly to bypass complex inquiries into whether prospective human plaintiffs have injuries in fact [required to attain standing]. Indeed, I believe that in some circumstances, Congress should do exactly that, to provide a supplement to limited public enforcement efforts.

It is worth noting that Sunstein's commitment to animal standing has been sustained over time. He made a similar argument in an article published in the *UCLA Law Review* in 2000. His support for animal rights also extends to an explicit proposal in a 2007 speech to outlaw hunting other than for food, stating, "That should be against the law. It's time now."

Letting Humans Sue on Behalf of Animals

The idea of giving animals standing seems to be growing on the political left, perhaps because it would be so harmful to business interests. Laurence H. Tribe, the eminent Harvard Law School professor, has spoken supportively of the concept. On February 8, 2000, less than a year before his Supreme Court appearance on behalf of Vice President Al Gore in the aftermath of the Florida vote controversy, Tribe delivered a speech praising animal rights lawyer Stephen Wise and arguing on behalf of granting animals the right to sue:

> Recognizing that animals themselves by statute as holders of rights would mean that they could sue in their own name and in their own right. . . . Such animals would have what is termed legal standing. Guardians would ultimately have to be appointed to speak for these

voiceless rights-holders, just as guardians are appointed today for infants, or for the profoundly retarded. . . . But giving animals this sort of "virtual voice" would go a long way toward strengthening the protection they will receive under existing laws and hopefully improved laws, and our constitutional history is replete with instances of such legislatively conferred standing.

But animal rights lawyers aren't waiting until the law is changed before enlisting animals as litigants. While these efforts have so far been turned back by the courts, they have received respectful hearings on appeal. In 2004, an environmental lawyer sued in the name of the "Cetacean Community"—allegedly consisting of all the world's whales, porpoises, and dolphins—seeking an injunction preventing the federal government from conducting underwater sonar tests. When a trial court found that the "Community" had no standing, the case was appealed to the Ninth Circuit Court of Appeals, where anything can happen. The court refused to grant the whales and dolphins standing, but in language that must have warmed every animal liberationist's heart, it stated that theoretically, animals could attain the right to sue:

It is obvious that an animal cannot function as a plaintiff in the same manner as a juridically competent human being. But we see no reason why Article III [of the U.S. Constitution] prevents Congress from authorizing suit in the name of an animal any more than it prevents suits brought in the name of artificial persons such as corporations, partnerships or trusts, and even ships, or of juridically incompetent persons such as infants, juveniles and mental incompetents.

Animals Are Human Property and as Such Can't Sue Their Owners

Of all the ubiquitous advocacy thrusts by animal rights advocates, obtaining legal standing for animals would be the most damaging—which makes Sunstein's appointment to the overseer of federal regulations so worrisome and Senator Chambliss's hold on the nomination so laudable. Chambliss plans to meet with the nominee personally "to provide him the opportunity to fully explain his views." Chambliss said:

> Professor Sunstein's recommendation that animals should be permitted to bring suit against their owners with human beings as their representatives, is astounding in its display of a total lack of common sense. American farmers and ranchers would face a tremendous threat from frivolous lawsuits. Even if claims against them were found to be baseless in court, they would still bear the financial costs of reckless litigation. That's a cost that would put most family farming and ranching operations out of business.

But animal standing would do more than just plunge the entire animal industry sector into chaos. In one fell swoop, it would both undermine the status of animals as property and elevate them with the force of law toward legal personhood. On an existential level, the

"We're suing you under the equal opportunities legislation for failure to represent <u>our</u> rights."

perceived exceptional importance of human life would suffer a staggering body blow by erasing one of the clear legal boundaries that distinguishes people from animals. This is precisely the future for which animal rights/liberationists devoutly yearn.

EVALUATING THE AUTHOR'S ARGUMENTS:

Smith quotes from several sources to support the points he makes in his essay. Make a list of everyone he quotes, including their credentials and the nature of their comments. Then, analyze how Smith uses these quotes—are they used to directly support his arguments? Or do they serve to point out the absurdity of a particular position? Explain whether you found the use of the viewpoint's quotes effective, and why.

Animals Should Not Be Treated as the Property of Humans

Patrick Battuello

"We long ago abandoned the concept of human chattel . . . it is time to reevaluate a property status for sentient and intelligent beings."

In the following viewpoint, Patrick Battuello argues that animals should not be regarded as human property. The problem Battuello has with treating animals as property is that everyone treats their property differently—while some people keep the things they own in good working order and give them care and attention, others are neglectful, wasteful, and disrespectful of their property. Lumping animals into the category of property puts them at risk for being neglected or mistreated, he says, and this is wrong because animals are emotional, logical, and skilled in ways that cars or bicycles are not. For example, Battuello says that dogs exhibit qualities similar to young humans. In his opinion, then, acts of cruelty toward such skilled animals should be viewed in the same way that acts of cruelty would be toward human children. He concludes that just as humans eventually realized that slavery was morally wrong, so too should they come to reject the treatment of animals as property.

Battuello is a writer, vegan, and animal rights activist who lives in upstate New York. He frequently blogs on these topics for the *Times Union,* a newspaper in Albany, New York.

AS YOU READ, CONSIDER THE FOLLOWING QUESTIONS:
1. According to Battuello, what are examples of rights that are exclusive to humans?
2. Who is Sandra Maurer, and how does she factor into the author's argument?
3. What is the "equal consideration of interests" as described by the author, and how does it factor into his argument?

When animal advocates speak of rights we are often derisively dismissed as fringe extremists who would have the audacity to accord total equality to nonhuman animals. This, of course, is a complete misinterpretation of the philosophy. Many rights are exclusive to humans (right to vote, to own property, to bear arms). But when I first read [a 2009 news story about animal cruelty in New York], I thought, what is it exactly that we are saying about these dogs? Do they not have a *right* not to suffer from intentional cruelty?

Humans Treat Animals Cruelly When They Are Only "Property"

Their *owner,* Sandra Maurer of Greene County, faces five counts of animal cruelty for failing to provide proper sustenance. Ronald Perez, President of the Columbia-Green Humane Society, said, *"So that's extremely emaciated. It doesn't get much worse than this other than death. They certainly wouldn't have made it through this winter in the condition they are in."* Maurer claims innocence and has hired a lawyer, apparently having funds for a legal defense but not food for her dogs. She faces misdemeanor charges. Deliberate cruelty to a sentient intelligent being is punishable by no more than one year in jail and/or a $1000 fine.

Since this case has yet to play out, allow me to introduce you to Joseph Gadomski, 61 at the time, who was arrested in February '02 for allowing his 14-year-old German Shepherd, Conan, to literally freeze to death in Albany in December '01. Conan was 50 pounds underweight and dragged his crippled hind legs when walking. The prosecutor, Eric Galarneau, said, *"He froze to the ground next to his water dish, which was completely frozen over. Nobody saw any food."* The judge in the case, William Carter, said, *"The only shelter I could see was a hole he had dug in the ground."* Judge Carter quoted the Animal Control Officer, Lenny Charbonneau, as saying, *"he never felt so bad for an animal."* For this, Gadomski was sentenced to 10 months in jail after rejecting a plea deal of 60 days and 3 years probation. Two months for torture and murder.

Penalties for Animal Mistreatment Are Too Lenient

Deborah Bradley, of Troy, was arrested last December for leaving her two-year -old Pit Bull in the backyard for over a month without food, water, or proper shelter. Troy Police Officer, James Bottillo, said, *"This dog suffered a horrible, painful, elongated death."* The vet who performed the necropsy [an autopsy performed on an animal] called the dog's condition "horrific". Bottillo said, *"When the vet was able to get into the dog's stomach, the contents in the dog's stomach were some rocks and sticks. . . ."* Troy PD spokesman, Dave Dean, said, *"I have no words to describe the sadness I feel when I consider the circumstances of this dog's death."* Bradley was charged with Aggravated Cruelty to Animals (Buster's Law, 1999), a felony, carrying only 1–2 years jail time. Octavia Latimer was charged under Buster's Law in the death of another Pit Bull in 2004. The dog was found *frozen to the ground.* Vernon Nix, of Troy, was arrested this past January for causing his emaciated dog to suffer brain damage due to hypothermia. He apparently forgot that his dog was chained outside in eight degree temperatures.

Animals Exhibit Many Human Qualities and Emotions

In philosophy, there exists the principle of *Equal Consideration of Interests.* Dogs have long been considered among the most intelligent of

Animal Abuse Is a Serious Problem

Thousands of animal abuse cases are filed each year, but not even a quarter of them lead to convictions. Animal rights activists say that because so many people mistreat their animals, it is wrong to view them as human property.

Animal Abuse Cases: 13,771 total

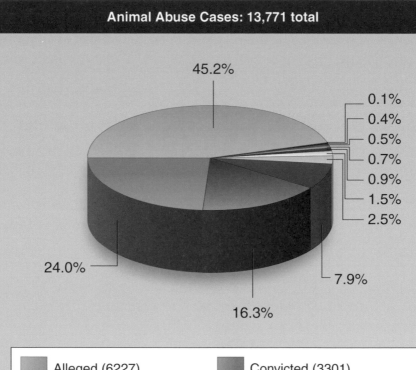

45.2%
0.1%
0.4%
0.5%
0.7%
0.9%
1.5%
2.5%
24.0%
7.9%
16.3%

Alleged (6227)
Convicted (3301)
Open (2245)
Not Charged (1088)
USDA Citation (351)
Dismissed (202)
Acquitted (125)
State Citation (102)
Civil Case (63)
Dismissed (Conditional) (49)
Failed to Appear (18)

Taken from: Pet-Abuse.com, 2010.

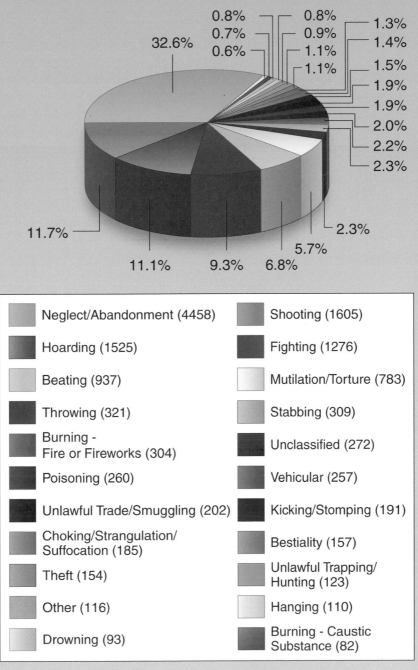

32.6%
0.8%
0.7%
0.6%
0.8%
0.9%
1.1%
1.1%
1.3%
1.4%
1.5%
1.9%
1.9%
2.0%
2.2%
2.3%
2.3%
5.7%
6.8%
9.3%
11.1%
11.7%

Neglect/Abandonment (4458)
Hoarding (1525)
Beating (937)
Throwing (321)
Burning - Fire or Fireworks (304)
Poisoning (260)
Unlawful Trade/Smuggling (202)
Choking/Strangulation/ Suffocation (185)
Theft (154)
Other (116)
Drowning (93)

Shooting (1605)
Fighting (1276)
Mutilation/Torture (783)
Stabbing (309)
Unclassified (272)
Vehicular (257)
Kicking/Stomping (191)
Bestiality (157)
Unlawful Trapping/ Hunting (123)
Hanging (110)
Burning - Caustic Substance (82)

Taken from: Pet-Abuse.com, 2010.

Research indicates the average dog is linguistically equal to a two-year-old human, arithmetically equal to a three- to four-year-old, and socially equal to a teenager.

animals. Stanley Coren, psychology professor and neuropsychological researcher at British Columbia University, is considered a leading expert on canine intelligence. He says, *"Their stunning flashes of brilliance and creativity are reminders that they may not be Einsteins but are sure closer to humans than we thought."* His research indicates the average dog is linguistically equivalent to a two-year old, arithmetically equivalent to a three- or four-year-old, and socially equivalent to a teenager. Other studies have demonstrated that dogs have spatial problem solving skills, locating valued items or operating latches and simple machines and, like toddlers, they obviously (at least to anyone who has shared a home with a dog) show basic emotions; happiness, anger, jealousy, fear, excitement etc. Coren says, *"They can also deliberately deceive, which is something the young children only start developing later in their life."* If dogs are on a par with small children or the mentally enfeebled, why do we not consider their interest in not being tortured or killed in the same way we do the aforementioned humans? Why are most animal cruelty laws misdemeanors when the Buster's Law felony [has] only a maximum two year sentence? What kind of human beings are Maurer, Gadomski, Bradley, Latimer, and Nix? Do their acts not define evil? Surely, their sentences (or possible sentences) do not represent justice. How would you feel if their acts were committed against a toddler? Intellectual consistency demands that we treat similar acts in a similar way. There should be no moral dividing line. Because of like physiologies and recognizable reactions to noxious stimuli, it should not be difficult to imagine the pain and suffering that these dogs experienced. The word is empathy.

We Can't Protect Animals Until We Treat Them as More than Property

Animals have a unique position within our society. While we readily acknowledge their capacity for pain and suffering, a characteristic that bonds humans and animals and no other known object in the universe, we still allow them to be regarded as property or resources. A resource, by its very nature, cannot have meaningful legal protection. This is the *moral schizophrenia* that Professor Francione refers to. Through the *Humane Treatment Principle,* that sets the standard for state anti-cruelty laws, our society concedes animal suffering and legislates against gross negligence and heinous cruelty that causes that suffering. Why then the probations, small fines, and light sentences? Because animals, pets in this case, are property. As a dog owner, I am legally required to provide minimum sustenance and shelter. But *I* place the value on my property. If I choose to keep my dog forever chained in the backyard or beat him for sullying the carpet, that is my prerogative. Property rights have a cherished status in our country. Francione says, *"The property status of animals renders completely meaningless any balancing that is supposedly required under the humane treatment principle or animal welfare laws,*

> **FAST FACT**
>
> According to the organization Born Free USA, more than 50 million animals are violently killed for use in fashion every year.

because what we really balance are the interests of property owners against the interests of their animal property. . . . We are generally reluctant to impose the stigma of criminal liability on property owners for what they do with the own property. . . ."

Animals Deserve to Be More Than Just Property

My position, that animals should never be human property, is extreme on the surface. But I believe it to be rationally and morally consistent. We long ago abandoned the concept of human chattel, and with our knowledge and appreciation of the animal mind growing with each passing year, it is time to reevaluate a property status for sentient and intelligent beings still influenced [by] the unenlightened theories of [seventeenth-century philosophers] Rene Descartes and John Locke. In addition, we could then punish the terrible people in this article with authority, and not be hampered with a *moral schizophrenia* conflict.

EVALUATING THE AUTHORS' ARGUMENTS:

To make his argument, Battuello compares the practice of owning animals to the practice of owning human slaves. What do you think each of the authors in this chapter would say about this comparison? Would they agree or disagree? Write one to two sentences on how you think each author might respond, and then state your own opinion.

Viewpoint 5

Giving Animals Rights Threatens Human Rights

Charles Colson and Anne Morse

"Instead of elevating human rights, this cause [animal rights] diminishes them by insisting we eliminate the distinction between humans and animals."

In the following viewpoint, Charles Colson and Anne Morse warn that granting rights to animals threatens to erode human rights. They argue that humans are unique in having souls, being conscious of their existence, and of bearing the image of God. They think these qualities separate them from animals in significant ways, and that rights should only be conferred upon creatures who possess these qualities. Colson and Morse warn that granting rights to animals not only reduces the uniqueness of human beings but also threatens society's well being. For example, if animals are no longer allowed to be used for research to find life-saving medicines, or if their products are no longer able to be used for human consumption, humans will suffer as a result. For all of these reasons, Colson and Morse think that conceding rights to animals threatens to put society down a slippery slope to devalue the uniqueness of the human soul and the quality of human society.

Colson is a former advisor to President Richard Nixon and a leading cultural commentator in the Christian right movement. He is also the founder of Prison Fellowship Ministries, a prison advocacy group for which Morse is a senior writer.

AS YOU READ, CONSIDER THE FOLLOWING QUESTIONS:
1. What are humans entitled to for having an eternal soul, in the authors' opinion?
2. In what ways do Christians act irrationally when it comes to their pets, according to Colson and Morse?
3. According to the authors, the animal rights movement is different from what other American social movements? In what way?

Five years ago I warned in this space about an aggressive animal-rights movement that seeks to blur the distinction between animals and humans. Since then it has gained steam, even unwittingly drawing some Christians into its orbit.

I know of a Bible study group in Los Angeles that recently laid hands on a sick dog, praying God would heal her—and if not, receive her into heaven. A Christian veterinarian administers healing sessions for patients. And dozens of websites offer biblical "proof" that animals are resurrected, as if Christ's atonement somehow included them.

Well-meaning evangelical authors write of their hopes that God will admit their beloved dogs into heaven: at Amazon.com, the list of books maintaining that pets are heaven-bound is long and furry. (My personal favorite: *Cold Noses at the Pearly Gates*, "a beautifully written book from a Christian perspective about our beloved pets" going to heaven.)

Are these merely examples of overzealous animal lovers—or signs of the latest "rights" campaign gaining steam?

Of course, Christians have a specific command to care for the creation. Genesis records that God, after forming every living creature

Charles Colson, former Watergate felon turned evangelist, believes that animals should not in any way be considered equal to humans because they have no soul.

and calling this "good," entrusts to Adam the task of ruling over them in a responsible way. William Wilberforce, demonstrating this duty, founded the Society for the Prevention of Cruelty to Animals in 1824. As such, we should delight in the unique joy that animals bring, and support the work of local shelters that care for abused and abandoned animals.

But that's not what we're witnessing here. These are signs of Christians weakening their best defense against activists on what constitutes the distinctiveness of humans.

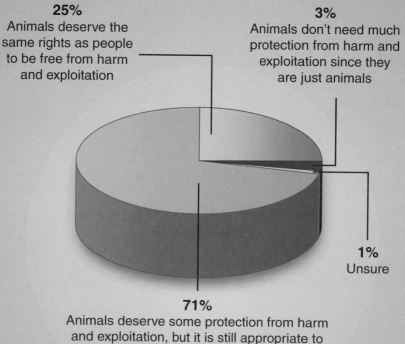

Americans View Animals as Animals, Not People

A 2008 Gallup poll found that the overwhelming majority of Americans believe that while animals should not be arbitrarily harmed, they do not deserve to be given rights in full.

25%
Animals deserve the same rights as people to be free from harm and exploitation

3%
Animals don't need much protection from harm and exploitation since they are just animals

1%
Unsure

71%
Animals deserve some protection from harm and exploitation, but it is still appropriate to use them for the benefit of humans

Taken from: Gallup poll, May 8–11, 2008.

Christianity teaches that humans are unique in all of creation: we are conscious of our existence, aware of death, capable of works of great creativity, and the only part of creation that bears the image of God. Humans alone have eternal souls, which confers unique moral status.

Many animal-rights activists dismiss any distinctions between humans and animals as "speciesism," which Princeton professor Peter Singer defines as "a prejudice" that favors "the interests of members of one's own species . . . against those of members of other species." If the material world is all there is, if humans are nothing more than the product of evolutionary forces, then they are essentially no different from pigs, dogs—or rats, as Ingrid Newkirk of PETA [People for the Ethical Treatment of Animals] once famously said. Humans are merely the latest stage in evolutionary development.

At least we should give PETA, Singer, and others credit for their consistency: their campaigns to grant constitutional rights to pigs or to make it illegal to keep laying hens in cages are perfectly logical. It is Christians who are behaving irrationally when they fall into naturalist positions out of love for their pets, even when our faith teaches that humans alone have eternal value.

The Scriptures tell us that animals are soulless creatures, and will perish with the rest of creation. We will not see them while our souls rest with God; when Christ returns and our bodies are resurrected, we will live in the new heavens and new earth—where there may be new, not resurrected, animals.

If we fail to understand our own doctrines, more and more Americans will begin to accept the idea that animals and humans are morally equivalent—and animal-rights activists may press on to their ultimate goals: eliminating animal agriculture and banning scientific research that uses animals—jeopardizing the development of life-saving medicines. And, as Singer proposes in his

> # FAST FACT
>
> In 2008, Spain was internationally criticized for its attempts to categorize Great Apes as persons and grant them the right to life and liberty. Many countries argued that it is inappropriate to grant human rights to animals when so many people in the world do not yet enjoy such rights.

utilitarian system of ethics, activists would seek to allocate scarce resources fairly among animals and humans. (Fido's operation will create greater happiness than keeping Uncle Ben on life support.)

You may think that no one would fall for Singer's preposterous arguments. But remember, throughout our history, Americans have engaged in great moral crusades, fighting against slavery, for suffrage, and for civil rights, which went against the grain of their times (and thank God Americans did). But the animal-rights cause is quite different: Instead of elevating human rights, this cause diminishes them by insisting we eliminate the distinction between humans and animals. It would be our moral undoing.

Christians, arguing that humans alone are made in God's image, can make a logical defense of the uniqueness of human life. But if out of sentimentality we treat our pets as if they have souls, we give away the argument. What a tragic irony if the church finds it has been conquered on behalf of our beloved pets.

EVALUATING THE AUTHORS' ARGUMENTS:

Colson and Morse use religious ideology to support their argument that granting rights to animals threatens the rights of humans. List at least three ways in which they do this. Then, state whether you agree with their reasoning. What pieces of evidence swayed you? With which pieces did you disagree?

Giving Animals Rights Does Not Threaten Human Rights

Josephine Donovan

"We have a moral responsibility to care for all creatures with whom we can communicate, regardless of how different they may be from us."

In the following viewpoint, Josephine Donovan argues that animals are entitled to rights, and granting them these rights does not take away from the rights that humans enjoy. She discusses different theories that offer ways to think about animals and their rights. Since humans can communicate relatively well with animals—in particular, understand when they feel pain—humans are morally obligated to take action to enhance animals' lives. Donovan says that through these communications, humans can be sure that animals do not want to be slaughtered, eaten, subjected to pain, or treated as objects. Humans have an obligation to grant them protection from these mistreatments in the form of rights. In her opinion, doing so does not diminish the status of humans—

rather, she concludes that humans are enhanced by the experience of treating animals compassionately and humanely.

Donovan is a professor at the University of Maine and the editor of *The Feminist Care Tradition in Animal Ethics.*

AS YOU READ, CONSIDER THE FOLLOWING QUESTIONS:
1. What is the feminist care approach to animal ethics, as described by Donovan?
2. What is the theory of "Cartesian dualism," and how does it factor into the author's argument?
3. When does Donovan think it is acceptable to override an animal's wishes?

Philosophical discussion about the moral status of animals intensified in sophistication and scope in the later decades of the twentieth century, thanks in part to groundbreaking works like Peter Singer's *Animal Liberation* (1975) and Tom Regan's *The Case for Animal Rights* (1983). The latter book especially helped to formulate the idea that aspects of the liberal "natural rights" doctrine, usually reserved for humans, should be applied to animals—hence the concept "animal rights," which is now broadly used to characterize the current animal defense movement.

The Equality of Creatures

Beginning in the 1980s, feminist theorists developed a feminist approach to the issue of the moral status of animals, or what is now termed "animal ethics." . . .

The feminist care approach to animal ethics . . . resists hierarchical dominative dualisms, which establish the powerful (humans, males, whites) over the subordinate (animals, women, people of color). Instead, care theorists see all living creatures as having value and as embedded in an interdependent matrix. . . .

In applying the feminist care ethic to animals, theorists argued that while natural rights theory makes important contributions to theorizing about animals, it nevertheless is in many ways inadequate and unworkable when applied to animals. . . .

We therefore need an ethic that acknowledges that nonhuman animals are different, are not in fact human, but are nevertheless entitled to moral respect. Care theory argues that we have a moral responsibility to care for all creatures with whom we can communicate, regardless of how different they may be from us. Of course, the degree to which active caring is possible will vary according to circumstances. For example, our responsibilities for domestic animals vary greatly from our duties to wild animals. . . .

Animals Are Individuals with Feelings, Needs, and Rights

The feminist ethic of care sees animals as individuals who do have feelings, who can communicate those feelings, and to whom therefore humans have moral obligations. An ethic of care also recognizes the diversity of animals—one size doesn't fit all; each has a particular history. Insofar as possible, attention needs to be paid to these particularities in any ethical determination regarding them.

One of the primary theories that continues to legitimize animal abuse is Cartesian dualism—the division of the world into mind and matter.

In the Cartesian view, matter is assumed to be lifeless and without energizing spirit (unlike in much premodern thinking, which is animist), and is held therefore to be of lesser value than mind, spirit, or reason. From this viewpoint, which undergirds much modern thinking about animals, which is instrumental, animals are reduced to mere things, machine-like automatons lacking inner spirit, sensitivity, or feelings. Thomas Kelch has pointed out that it is this view that supports the current common-law conception of animals as property. Kelch argues that reconceptualizing the moral status of animals as feeling subjects will require changing the legal status of animals.

> **FAST FACT**
>
> One of the first advocates for animal rights was Lewis Gompertz, who in 1824 was a founding member of the Society for the Prevention of Cruelty to Animals.

Like feminism in general, feminist care theory is a political theory and is therefore unlike traditional welfare approaches to animal issues,

Care theorists argue that humans have a moral responsibility to care for all creatures with whom they can communicate no matter how different they are from themselves.

which deal with one animal at a time and fail to critique or oppose the system responsible. Ethic-of-care theory insists that these causal systems be addressed. As Catharine MacKinnon has noted, we're for "caring and empathy while never letting power off the hook."

The feminist care approach therefore pays *attention* (a key word in feminist ethic-of-care theorizing) not only to the individual suffering animal but also to the political and economic systems that are causing the suffering. The feminist care approach in short recognizes the importance of each individual animal while also developing a more comprehensive analysis of why the animal is being abused in the first place. . . .

We Can Interact Meaningfully with Animals

Recently, some ethic-of-care theorists have proposed that our attention should be directed as well to what the animals are telling us about themselves, rather than what other humans are telling us about them. In my article "Caring to Dialogue," I have called for a renewed emphasis on dialogue with animals, learning their communication systems, reading their body language phenomenologically, and taking these communications seriously in our ethical decisions.

Such communication may be imperfect. It may indeed be impossible to really know, as Thomas Nagel famously put it, "what it is like to be a bat" (1974). But we can nevertheless decipher animal communications sufficiently to formulate an appropriate ethical response. Indeed, we use the same mental and emotional operations in reading an animal as wc do a human. Body language, eye movement, facial expression, and tone of voice all are important signs. One might in fact argue that nonhuman animals' emotional responses are more clear and direct than humans' and thus are easier to read. In reading animals it is sometimes helpful to know about species' habits and culture. And as with humans, repeated experiences with one individual help one to understand that individual's unique needs and wishes.

Humans Should Respect Animals' Wishes

One of the principal ways by which one understands animal "language" sympathetically is by analogy to one's own experience. Say I saw a dog yelping, whining, leaping about, and licking an open cut. Because under similar circumstances I know I would likewise feel like crying and moving about anxiously because of the pain, I therefore conclude that the animal is experiencing the same kind of pain as I would. Knowing that one would wish one's own pain to be alleviated, one is moved to do the same for the animal. Of course, the animal's expressed feelings or wishes cannot always be determinative. At times humans may have to override them for their own good (as when one vaccinates one's companion animal). And to be sure the more different the creature is from oneself the more difficult the communication. But even insects, fish, reptiles, and birds react in ways we can relate to: avoiding pain and threats of death, and seeking that which enhances their life.

Respecting Animals Does Not Diminish Humans' Status

If, in short, we really begin to pay attention to what other creatures are telling us, we will hear that they do not want to be slaughtered, eaten, subjected to pain, or treated instrumentally as unfeeling objects. It behooves us humans as ethical beings to incorporate their wishes when we make decisions—as we inevitably must—about their lives.

EVALUATING THE AUTHORS' ARGUMENTS:

Josephine Donovan and Charles Colson and Anne Morse (authors of the previous viewpoint) agree that humans have an obligation to treat animals compassionately. Yet they disagree that this means animals should be granted rights. Write a paragraph that explains each position, and then state with which position you ultimately agree. Identify two key pieces of evidence that helped sway you—these can be quotes, facts, or ideas posited by the authors.

Viewpoint

7

The Goals of Animal Rights Activists Are Extreme

P. Michael Conn

"Is 'knuckle-headed' really the right description for those who place bombs at researchers' residences or under their cars?"

In the following viewpoint P. Michael Conn explains why he thinks the activities of animal rights activists are extreme. Although Conn believes that animals should not be arbitrarily abused or neglected, he does not think they should be granted the same status as humans. Animal rights activists, on the other hand, believe that animals are enslaved by humans and make it their responsibility to release them from this bondage. Conn describes how, to this end, animal rights activists have threatened researchers and their families with violence and set fire to multiple laboratories where research involving animals took place. Because they broke the law in defense of their political beliefs, and used scare tactics to force professionals to abandon their research, Conn considers such activists to be terrorists. He warns that legitimizing the animal rights cause will only encourage more acts of terrorism to take place.

P. Michael Conn, "Terrorism in the Name of Animal Rights," *Los Angeles Times*, November 12, 2008. Copyright © 2008 *Los Angeles Times*. Reproduced by permission of the author.

Conn is a professor and research director at the Oregon Health and Science University's Oregon National Primate Center and coauthor of the book *The Animal Research War*.

AS YOU READ, CONSIDER THE FOLLOWING QUESTIONS:
1. Who is Elliot Katz, and how does he factor into Conn's argument?
2. What is the Animal Enterprise Terrorism Act, as described by the author?
3. Why does the author think the word "knucklehead" is not strong enough to describe the actions of animal rights activists?

Words convey more than concepts; they stir up our feelings and direct our thoughts. Racial and religious epithets have started riots, and calling the police officer who pulls your speeding car over "Sir" is a smart way for you to start the conversation.

Animal rights activists know how important words can be. The Northern California-based organization In Defense of Animals and its founder, Elliot Katz, advocate substituting "companion animal" for "pet" and "animal guardian" for "pet owner" in local ordinances and everyday parlance. The idea is "to elicit responsible treatment of companion animals and end abuse, neglect and abandonment of pets."

Going Too Far with Animal Rights

Well, OK, it's never right to abuse or neglect animals, but U.S. law already contains vigorously enforced animal welfare statutes that require animals to be fed, sheltered and treated as more than just property. It is legal to toss an old coat in a dumpster, but it is not legal to toss an old dog into one.

So if we already distinguish animals from property, why do we need word changes in public ordinances? Probably because many animal rights activists want more. They want to persuade us that animals deserve nearly equal rights with people. "Rights-holders," of course, couldn't be "enslaved" as pets, nor could they be used in scientific research.

I'm a researcher and director of research advocacy at the Oregon Health and Science University, where humane, federally regulated

A Timeline of Animal Rights Terrorism

Some animal rights groups—such as the Animal Liberation Front (ALF) and the Earth Liberation Front (ELF)—are regarded by the U.S. government as terrorist groups. Actions committed by members of these and other animal rights groups range from petty pranks and vandalism to bombings, threats, and attempted murder.

2009

November 5, 2009 Kansas City, MO: ALF members vandalize a meat packing company by covering five trucks with spray paint, gluing locks, slashing tires, and pouring sugar in gas tanks.

September 6, 2009 Miami, FL: ALF members slash tires and pour red paint over the car and home of an importer of primates for biomedical research.

June 16, 2009 Portland, OR: Animal rights activists vandalize the Nicholas Ungar Furs store by spreading red paint on the building, windows, signs, and sidewalks.

March 7, 2009 Los Angeles, CA: ALF members firebomb the car of a UCLA neuroscientist using a homemade incendiary device.

January 10, 2009 Davis, CA: Animal rights activists send letter bombs to two UC Davis primate researchers.

January 8, 2009 Los Angeles, CA: A group calling itself "Justice Department" sends a greeting card containing razor blades coated with blood and rat poison to a UCLA primate researcher.

2008

December 29, 2008 Baltimore, MD: ALF members send letter bombs to two primate researchers at Johns Hopkins University.

December 9, 2008 Berkeley, CA: ALF members send a computer virus, embedded in an e-mail, to various workers at the Visual Neuroscience Laboratory at Berkeley.

November 27, 2008 Los Angeles, CA: ELF activists glue locks and spray-paint graffiti at a UCLA medical clinic.

August 19, 2008 South Jordan, UT: Animal rights activists break into a mink farm, release about 650 mink, and destroy breeding records.

August 2, 2008 Santa Cruz, CA: Animal rights terrorists throw Molotov cocktail bombs at a car parked outside the campus home of a UCSC researcher. A few minutes later another researcher's home is firebombed, forcing the man, his wife, and two young children to escape on a fire ladder from the second story.

March 20, 2008 Delhi, NY: A group calling itself ARF (Animal Rights Front, Inc.) claims responsibility for an arson fire that destroys a taxidermy shop.

February 24, 2008 Westside, Santa Cruz, CA: An attempted home invasion by six masked animal rights activists occurred at the home of a UCSC faculty member who uses mice in breast cancer research.

2007

August 5, 2007, Maryland: ALF activists destroy eight boats entered in a sport fishing tournament. They used scuba divers to weld propellers and cut holes below the waterline.

Taken from: National Animal Interest Alliance (NAIA), 2010.

animal research is conducted. I don't believe that animals should be treated as the ethical coequals of people. One way to understand the issue is to carry the underlying logic to its extreme: Would you extend to the surviving family of a rabbit the right to sue the fox that killed it? Should a monkey have the right to sue, or have a lawsuit brought on its behalf against a research lab?

Just as Katz's group and others care what words describe pets, I care what words are used to describe animal rights activists. Some, I believe, deserve to be called "terrorists."

"I Felt Terrorized"

In 2001, when I interviewed for a position at a Florida university, I was publicly and privately harassed, followed, threatened and accused of lying about the fact that my own research didn't use animals. A police officer had to be assigned to protect me. Later, the FBI found my name and address among the papers of a man who was arrested for trespassing at the Oregon Health and Science University, a man whose website described how to make firebombs. I can assure you that I felt terrorized.

Much worse has happened to others. Four of my colleagues have received letters "armed" with razors set to cut the hands of anyone who opened them. In August [2008], scientists at UC Santa Cruz and their families survived firebombings, and UCLA researchers have been similarly attacked.

Extremists have even posted pictures of scientists' children on their incendiary websites in order to get the scientists to stop animal research. In some cases, they've succeeded.

When Activism Turns Violent

Of course, the leaders of a few animal rights organizations decry violence and criminal acts, and even the movement's more shadowy

Animal rights protesters have committed violent acts in pursuit of their cause, such as this defacement of a University of California researcher's home.

groups often claim that they act on the first principle of protecting human and animal life. But the law increasingly sees the movement's extreme actions for what they are.

When 10 activists were convicted of arsons committed from 1995 to 2001 throughout the West (responsibility for the actions was claimed by the Animal Liberation Front and the Earth Liberation

Front), U.S. District Judge Ann Aiken applied "terrorism enhancements" that increased sentences for the defendants.

In November 2006, the federal Animal Enterprise Terrorism Act was signed into law by President Bush, creating tough penalties for damaging property, making threats and conspiring against zoos, research labs and similar enterprises.

Many on both sides of the issue took note of the use of the "T-word" in the name of the act. The science journal *Nature* bristled. "Calling someone a terrorist is a value judgment," it said in an unsigned editorial. While some "knuckleheaded actions could easily have accidentally hurt someone, [the] ethos was to damage property, never to hurt or kill."

Animal Rights Activists Should Be Considered Terrorists

Which brings us back to words. Is "knuckleheaded" really the right description for those who place bombs at researchers' residences or under their cars? Is it the right word for targeting children to press their parents to give up animal research?

The terrorist tag is sticking. Just as laws in West Hollywood, San Jose, San Francisco and other cities now term pets "companion animals," federal law is increasingly viewing those who use violence or intimidate by threat of violence as terrorists.

The extremists in the movement will not and should not be able to shed this label unless they rethink their tactics and strategies.

EVALUATING THE AUTHOR'S ARGUMENTS:

The author of this viewpoint, P. Michael Conn, is a researcher who has been threatened and harassed by animal rights activists. Does the fact that he has personal experience with this issue influence your opinion of his argument? If so, in what way?

The Goals of Animal Rights Activists Are Not Extreme

"People who [participated in] activities associated with constitutionally protected ... free speech found themselves facing prosecution as 'terrorists.'"

Justin Goodman

In the following viewpoint, Justin Goodman argues that people who stick up for the rights of animals are unjustly branded as terrorists. He recounts how animal rights activists have been imprisoned and called terrorists for participating in activities that are part of each American's right to free speech—such as the right to nonviolently protest, the right to disseminate information, and the right to speak in public about issues and actions they feel passionately about. Goodman says that the goals of animal rights activists are noble—they are merely standing up for animals that are tortured and even killed in the process of research. In Goodman's opinion, not only is such research unethical, but people who protest against it are reasonable, ethical, and have a constitutional right to do so.

Goodman is a research associate supervisor for the People for the Ethical Treatment of Animals. He also teaches in Marymount University's Department of Sociology and Criminal Justice.

AS YOU READ, CONSIDER THE FOLLOWING QUESTIONS:
1. What does the term "civil disobedience" mean in the context of the viewpoint?
2. What does the author say were the findings of an eight-month undercover investigation at the University of Utah? Name at least three findings.
3. How, according to Goodman, are researchers and protesters treated differently by the government?

I n the last few years — ever since the passage of the chilling Animal Enterprise Terrorism Act and the implementation of an earlier incarnation of the law — the free speech rights of some animal activists have been trampled in McCarthy-like fashion.[1]

Nonviolent Protesters Are Being Treated Like Terrorists

People who spoke at public events about the torment that animals are forced to endure in laboratories, sent faxes in protest, ran an informational Web site and organized and attended protests on public property — activities associated with constitutionally protected free speech — found themselves facing prosecution as "terrorists."

This should give all Americans pause. People who engage in nonviolent protests and civil disobedience are sitting in jail cells, stigmatized by one of the most politically charged and discrediting labels of our time, while people who wake up every morning and go to jobs in which they torment and kill animals in laboratories continue to enjoy their freedom, paychecks, social lives and families.

A Legitimate Cause to Protest

As a case in point, PETA just released the findings of an eight-month undercover investigation at the University of Utah in Salt Lake City.

---

1. The author is referring to Senator Joseph McCarthy, who investigated Americans suspected of Communist treason and disloyalty in the 1950s.

Wearing a hidden camera, our investigator documented circumstances that violate our moral sensibilities about how we ought to treat animals and represent what we believe are dozens of violations of federal laws and guidelines governing the treatment of dogs, cats, rabbits, monkeys, mice, rats and pigs.

Tiny mice with grotesque tumors were left to suffer from cancers that had nearly grown bigger than their bodies. Laboratory workers couldn't even manage to make sure that all mice had water, and one worker admitted that mice in the laboratory die of dehydration "all the time."

Monkeys were kept deprived of water so that they would cooperate during experiments in exchange for a sip. Imagine these animals' lives: They had holes drilled into their skulls and metal hardware at-

tached to their heads. They live in tiny cages, all alone, without even the touch and comfort of a companion. They are so emotionally and physically traumatized that they constantly whirl or rock back and forth. And on top of all this, they are always thirsty — so thirsty they'll do almost anything for a few drops of water.

Getting Away with Murder — Literally

Our investigation also revealed that shelters near Salt Lake City sell dogs and cats to this university as though they were disposable laboratory equipment. Our investigator's video footage shows dogs at the shelter wagging their tails as lab techs approach their cages to assess whether they'd be good "subjects," unaware of the invasive, painful tests that are about to be conducted on them. This is a betrayal of these vulnerable animals and also of the public, which counts on animal shelters to be havens for homeless animals.

So think about it. People who drown, burn, cut open, shock, poison, starve, forcibly restrain, addict and inflict brain damage on helpless animals — whose only "offense" is that they weren't born human —are walking among us, being granted tenure and promotions and

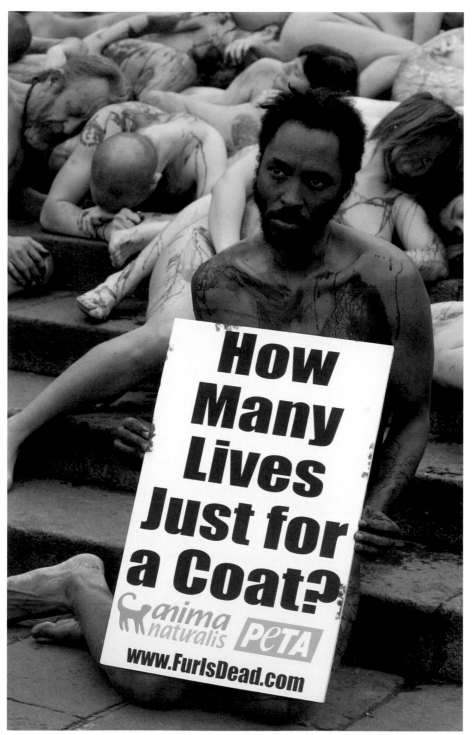

Animal rights activists put on an elaborate—yet peaceful—demonstration to protest the use of fur.

receiving huge chunks of our tax dollars to bankroll their cruel and crude experiments. On the frequent occasions when they violate federal animal welfare laws in their laboratories, the government usually just asks them to pinky swear not to do it again. Meanwhile, compassionate people who are willing to speak up about one of the great injustices of our time and use nonviolent protest tactics to effect change for animals may be locked up.

It Is Every American's Right to Protest

Like all other citizens and businesses, companies and people who abuse animals are already protected from violence and criminal acts by state and federal laws that have been used effectively by police and prosecutors to punish people who engage in illegal conduct against them. To shield them from public opinion and discussion and to protect them from peaceful and heretofore lawful pickets by locking up those who dare to challenge the suffering that occurs inside laboratories is an attack on every American's right of protest.

EVALUATING THE AUTHORS' ARGUMENTS:

Justin Goodman argues that animal rights activists are merely exercising their right to free speech. How do you think P. Michael Conn, author of the previous viewpoint, would respond to this claim? Write two to three sentences on what you think Conn would say. Then, state with which author you ultimately agree. Are the goals of animal rights activists extreme or reasonable? In your opinion, do they have the right to freely oppose animal research, or do they take their opposition too far?

Chapter 2

How Should Animals Be Treated?

Animal rights advocates in Seoul, South Korea, protest the making of dog meat soup, a traditional dish.

Viewpoint

1

It Is Unethical to Treat Animals as Food

Jonathan Safran Foer

"Our taboo against dog eating says something about dogs and a great deal about us."

In the following viewpoint, Jonathan Safran Foer argues it is wrong to eat animals. He proves this by considering the case of dog meat. He suggests that the only reason Americans do not eat dog is because it is not culturally acceptable to do so—Americans see dogs as companions rather than as food. But Foer argues there is no real reason they do not eat dog: after all, dogs share similar mental faculties as pigs, which are eaten in abundance. Also, eating dog could solve the social problems of hunger and stray animals. Foer concludes that Americans do not eat dog only because the idea of doing so disgusts them. But he argues if they really thought about it, Americans would also be disgusted by the thought of eating the flesh of any animal, even those that have become culturally acceptable to eat. He concludes that cultural acceptance

Jonathan Safran Foer, "Let Them Eat Dog: A Modest Proposal for Tossing Fido in the Oven," *The Wall Street Journal*, October 31, 2009. Copyright © 2009 Dow Jones & Company, Inc. All rights reserved. Reprinted with permission of *The Wall Street Journal*.

of meat eating has blinded Americans to the truth about meat, where it comes from, and the immorality of eating it.

Foer is the author of the novels *Everything Is Illuminated* and *Incredibly Loud and Close*. He has also written the non-fiction book *Eating Animals*.

AS YOU READ, CONSIDER THE FOLLOWING QUESTIONS:

1. What qualities does Foer say are shared by dogs, pigs, cows, and chickens?
2. What, according to Foer, has been described as "buttery" and "floral"?
3. What does Foer mean when he describes food as "not rational"? How does that description support his argument?

Despite the fact that it's perfectly legal in 44 states, eating "man's best friend" is as taboo as a man eating his best friend. Even the most enthusiastic carnivores won't eat dogs. TV guy and sometimes cooker Gordon Ramsay can get pretty macho with lambs and piglets when doing publicity for something he's selling, but you'll never see a puppy peeking out of one of his pots. And though he once said he'd electrocute his children if they became vegetarian, one can't help but wonder what his response would be if they poached the family pooch.

Dogs are wonderful, and in many ways unique. But they are remarkably unremarkable in their intellectual and experiential capacities. Pigs are every bit as intelligent and feeling, by any sensible definition of the words. They can't hop into the back of a Volvo, but they can fetch, run and play, be mischievous and reciprocate affection. So why don't they get to curl up by the fire? Why can't they at least be spared being tossed on the fire? Our taboo against dog eating says something about dogs and a great deal about us.

The French, who love their dogs, sometimes eat their horses.

The Spanish, who love their horses, sometimes eat their cows.

The Indians, who love their cows, sometimes eat their dogs.

While written in a much different context, George Orwell's words (from "Animal Farm") apply here: "All animals are equal, but some animals are more equal than others."

So who's right? What might be the reasons to exclude canine from the menu? The selective carnivore suggests:

Don't eat companion animals. But dogs aren't kept as companions in all of the places they are eaten. And what about our petless neighbors? Would we have any right to object if they had dog for dinner?

OK, then: Don't eat animals with significant mental capacities. If by "significant mental capacities" we mean what a dog has, then good for the dog. But such a definition would also include the pig, cow and chicken. And it would exclude severely impaired humans.

Then: It's for good reason that the eternal taboos—don't fiddle with your crap, kiss your sister, or eat your companions—are taboo. Evolutionarily speaking, those things are bad for us. But dog eating isn't a taboo in many places, and it isn't in any way bad for us. Properly cooked, dog meat poses no greater health risks than any other meat.

Dog meat has been described as "gamey" "complex," "buttery" and "floral." And there is a proud pedigree of eating it. Fourth-century tombs contain depictions of dogs being slaughtered along with other food animals. It was a fundamental enough habit to have informed language itself: the Sino-Korean character for "fair and proper" (yeon) literally translates into "as cooked dog meat is delicious." Hippocrates praised dog meat as a source of strength. Dakota Indians enjoyed dog liver, and not so long ago Hawaiians ate dog brains and blood. Captain Cook ate dog. Roald Amundsen famously ate his sled dogs. (Granted, he was really hungry.) And dogs are still eaten to overcome bad luck in the Philippines; as medicine in China and Korea; to enhance libido in Nigeria and in numerous places, on every continent,

FAST FACT

Erin E. Williams and Margo DeMello, authors of the book *Why Animals Matter*, report that each year, about 10 billion animals are killed in 5,700 slaughterhouses across the United States.

because they taste good. For centuries, the Chinese have raised special breeds of dogs, like the black-tongued chow, for chow, and many European countries still have laws on the books regarding postmortem examination of dogs intended for human consumption.

Vegetarians Have Their Reasons

About 4 percent of the U.S. population (6–8 million adults) is vegetarian. A poll of vegetarians yielded the following about why they chose to not eat meat.

"What was your most important reason for becoming a vegetarian?"

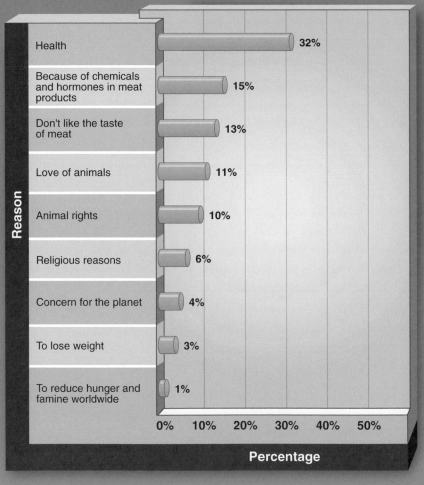

Taken from: *Time*/CNN, July 15, 2002.

Of course, something having been done just about everywhere is no kind of justification for doing it now. But unlike all farmed meat, which requires the creation and maintenance of animals, dogs are practically begging to be eaten. Three to four million dogs and cats are euthanized annually. The simple disposal of these euthanized dogs is an enormous ecological and economic problem. But eating those strays, those runaways, those not-quite-cute-enough-to-take and not-quite-well-behaved-enough-to-keep dogs would be killing a flock of birds with one stone and eating it, too.

In a sense it's what we're doing already. Rendering—the conversion of animal protein unfit for human consumption into food for livestock and pets—allows processing plants to transform useless dead dogs into productive members of the food chain. In America, millions of dogs and cats euthanized in animal shelters every year become the food for our food. So let's just eliminate this inefficient and bizarre middle step.

This need not challenge our civility. We won't make them suffer any more than necessary. While it's widely believed that adrenaline makes dog meat taste better—hence the traditional methods of slaughter: hanging, boiling alive, beating to death—we can all agree that if we're going to eat them, we should kill them quickly and painlessly, right? For example, the traditional Hawaiian means of holding the dog's nose shut—in order to conserve blood—must be regarded (socially if not legally) as a no-no. Perhaps we could include dogs under the Humane Methods of Slaughter Act. That doesn't say anything about how they're treated during their lives, and isn't subject to any meaningful oversight or enforcement, but surely we can rely on the industry to "self-regulate," as we do with other eaten animals.

Few people sufficiently appreciate the colossal task of feeding a world of billions of omnivores who demand meat with their potatoes. The inefficient use of dogs—conveniently already in areas of high human population (take note, local-food advocates)—should make any good ecologist blush. One could argue that various "humane" groups are the worst hypocrites, spending enormous amounts of money and energy in a futile attempt to reduce the number of unwanted dogs while at the very same time propagating the irresponsible no-dog-for-dinner taboo. If we let dogs be dogs, and breed without

A chef prepares the traditional Korean dish dog meat soup in a restaurant in Seoul. Eating dog is taboo in America but is acceptable in other societies.

interference, we would create a sustainable, local meat supply with low energy inputs that would put even the most efficient grass-based farming to shame. For the ecologically-minded it's time to admit that dog is realistic food for realistic environmentalists.

For those already convinced, here's a classic Filipino recipe I recently came across. I haven't tried it myself, but sometimes you can read a recipe and just know.

Stewed Dog, Wedding Style

First, kill a medium-sized dog, then burn off the fur over a hot fire. Carefully remove the skin while still warm and set aside for later (may be used in other recipes). Cut meat into 1" cubes. Marinate meat in mixture of vinegar, peppercorn, salt, and garlic for 2 hours. Fry meat in oil using a large wok over an open fire, then add onions and chopped pineapple and sauté until tender. Pour in tomato sauce and boiling water, add green pepper, bay leaf, and Tabasco. Cover and simmer over warm coals until meat is tender. Blend in purée of dog's liver and cook for additional 5–7 minutes.

There is an overabundance of rational reasons to say no to factory-farmed meat: It is the No. 1 cause of global warming, it systematically forces tens of billions of animals to suffer in ways that would be illegal if they were dogs, it is a decisive factor in the development of swine and avian flus, and so on. And yet even most people who know these things still aren't inspired to order something else on the menu. Why?

Food is not rational. Food is culture, habit, craving and identity. Responding to factory farming calls for a capacity to care that dwells beyond information. We know what we see on undercover videos of factory farms and slaughterhouses is wrong. (There are those who will defend a system that allows for occasional animal cruelty, but no one defends the cruelty, itself.) And despite it being entirely reasonable, the case for eating dogs is likely repulsive to just about every reader of this paper. The instinct comes before our reason, and is more important.

EVALUATING THE AUTHOR'S ARGUMENTS:

Rather than arguing straightforwardly that eating meat is wrong, Foer takes a creative approach to his argument. He uses an extreme case—eating dog meat—to argue that feeling repulsed by the thought of eating *some* types of meat should be grounds for feeling repulsed by the thought of eating *all* meat. In your opinion, was this an effective way of arguing his point? Do you ultimately agree with him? Explain your reasoning.

Viewpoint 2

Eating Meat Is Ethical

Christine Lennon

In the following viewpoint, Christine Lennon argues that meat can be a moral and healthy choice. She describes the increasing popularity of meat that comes from animals raised on small local farms. On these farms, animals are treated humanely, not given hormones or antibiotics, and produce minimal waste. In Lennon's opinion, these factors make it ethical to eat. She also argues that eating this meat is healthier than eating vegetarian meals that are highly processed, are loaded with fat and carbohydrates, and contain fewer whole nutrients. She concludes that the availability of locally raised meat makes it both a moral and nutritionally sound choice.

Lennon is a writer whose work has appeared in *InStyle, Time,* and *Food and Wine* magazine, where this viewpoint was originally published.

> *"The ethical reasons for eating meat, combined with the health-related ones, have been impossible to deny."*

AS YOU READ, CONSIDER THE FOLLOWING QUESTIONS:
  1. What do the terms "grass-fed" and "pasture raised" mean in the context of the viewpoint?
  2. In what way does the author say meat is healthier than vegetarian meals made with soy and wheat gluten?
  3. Who is Mollie Katzen and how does she factor into the author's argument?

To a die-hard meat eater, there's nothing more irritating than a smug vegetarian. I feel at liberty to say this because I am one (a steak lover) and I married the other (a vegetarian with a pulpit). For me, "Do you now, or would you ever, eat meat?" has always been a question on par with "Do you ever want to get married?" and "Do you want children?" The answer to one reveals as much about a person's interior life, and our compatibility, as the response to the others. My husband Andrew's reply to all of those questions when I asked him three years ago was, "No."

Obviously, we're now married. We had twins earlier this year. And somewhere in between those two events, the answer to the third question was also re-evaluated, and the vegetarian soapbox was put to rest, too.

The Conversion of a Vegetarian

Yes, my husband has started eating meat again after a seven-year hiatus as an ethically motivated and health-conscious vegetarian. About a year ago, we arrived at a compromise: I would eat less meat—choosing mostly beef, pork and poultry produced by local California ranchers without the use of hormones or antibiotics—and he would indulge me by sharing a steak on occasion. But arriving at that happy medium wasn't as straightforward as it sounds. In the three years we've been together, several turns of events have made both of us rethink our choices and decide that eating meat selectively is better for the planet and our own health. And judging by the conversations we've had with friends and acquaintances, we're not the only ones who believe this to be true.

For Andrew and about a dozen people in our circle who have recently converted from vegetarianism, eating sustainable meat purchased from small farmers is a new form of activism—a way of striking a blow against the factory farming of livestock that books like Michael Pollan's *The Omnivore's Dilemma* describe so damningly. Pollan extols the virtues of independent, small-scale food producers who raise pasture-fed livestock in a sustainable and ethical manner. In contrast, he provides a compelling critique of factory farms, which cram thousands of cows, pigs or chickens into rows of cages in warehouses, feed them drugs to plump up their meat and fight off the illnesses caused by these inhumane conditions, and produce innumerable tons of environmentally destructive animal waste.

An Example of Ethically Produced Meat

The terms "grass fed" and "pasture raised"—meaning that an animal was allowed to graze the old-fashioned way instead of being fed an unnatural and difficult-to-digest diet of mostly corn and other grain—have now entered the food-shoppers' lexicon. But Andrew and I didn't fully understand what those phrases meant until we got to know Greg Nauta of Rocky Canyon Farms. Nauta is a small-scale rancher and farmer from Atascadero, California, who grows organic vegetables and raises about 35 animals on pastureland. Since we met him at the Hollywood Farmers' Market a year ago, it has become even clearer to us that supporting guys like him—by seeking out and paying a premium for sustainably raised meat—is the right thing for us to do.

Nauta's cattle graze on 200 leased acres of pasture in central California and are fed the leftover vegetables and fruits he grows that don't sell at the farmers' market, supplemented by locally grown barley grain on occasion. "That's dessert," he says of the barley, "not a main course. That would be like us eating ice cream every day."

Three times a week, Nauta loads his truck full of coolers stocked with cattleman's steaks and handmade pork sausages and drives to the Los Angeles–area farmers' markets. Selling his vegetables and meat directly to conscientious eaters, people to whom he talks weekly about rainfall averages and organic produce, Nauta says, is "the best way small guys like me can compete." In the past several months, Nauta has noticed a handful of curious vegetarians, like Andrew, wandering

Pasture-raised beef has found a niche among consumers who prefer their beef not be raised in factory farms.

over to his booth to ask questions. And they're satisfied enough with the answers to give his meat a try—and come back for more.

The Nutritional Advantages of Meat

If preserving small-scale farming isn't a compelling enough reason to eat beef or pork, consider the nutritional advantages grass-fed meat has over the factory-fed kind. "One of the benefits of all-grass-fed beef, or 'beef with benefits,' as we say, is that it's lower in fat than conventionally raised beef," says Kate Clancy, who studies nutrition and sustainable agriculture and was until recently the senior scientist at the nonprofit Union of Concerned Scientists. "The other thing is that the meat and milk from grass-fed cattle will probably have higher amounts of omega-3 fatty acids, which may help reduce the risk of heart disease and strengthen people's immune systems. What's good for the environment, what's good for cattle, is also good for us."

Combine these findings with the questions being raised about meat replacements derived from soy and wheat gluten, and the real thing seems better by the minute. "What we know about soy is that as you process it, you lose a lot of the benefits," says Ashley Koff, a Los Angeles–based registered dietician. "Any soy-based fake meat product is incredibly processed, and you have to use chemicals to get the mock flavor. Any other whole-food diet is going to be a lot better for you." Vegetarians like Andrew—he once brought a tofu sandwich to a famous Texas barbecue restaurant—may now have a harder time justifying their "healthier" dietary choices.

"When I Eat Meat, I Feel More Grounded"

Former vegetarians are some of the most outspoken proponents of eating meat. "I was vegan for 16 years, and I truly believed I was doing the right thing for my health," says the actress and model Mariel Hemingway, who is the author of *Healthy Living from the Inside Out*. "But when I was vegan, I was super-weak. I love animals, and we should not support anything but ethical ranching, but when I eat meat, I feel more grounded. I have more energy."

Even chef Mollie Katzen, author of the vegetarian bible the *Moosewood Cookbook*, is experimenting with meat again. "For about 30 years I didn't eat meat at all, just a bite of fish every once in a while, and always some dairy," she says. "Lately, I've been eating a little meat. People say, 'Ha, ha, Mollie, Katzen is eating steak.' But now that cleaner, naturally fed meat is available, it's a great option for anyone who's looking to complete his diet. Somehow, it got ascribed to me that I don't want people to eat meat. I've just wanted to supply possibilities that were low on the food chain."

FAST FACT

A study done by a professor at Oklahoma State University Department of Agricultural Economics examined how people value the suffering of farm animals versus the suffering of one human. The suffering of one human was found to be equivalent to the suffering of 11,500 farm animals.

Recently, when responding to the invitation to her high-school reunion, Katzen had to make a choice between the vegetarian and the conventional meal. She checked the nonvegetarian box. "The people who requested the vegetarian meal got fettuccine Alfredo," she says. "It's a

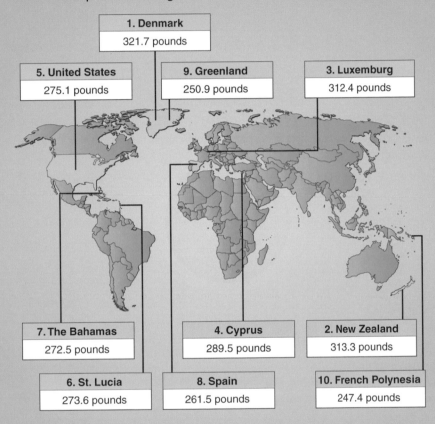

Meat Is Popular Worldwide

The U.S. ranks fifth on the top ten list of meat-eating countries, with each person eating about 275 lbs of meat per year.

1. Denmark
321.7 pounds

5. United States
275.1 pounds

9. Greenland
250.9 pounds

3. Luxemburg
312.4 pounds

7. The Bahamas
272.5 pounds

4. Cyprus
289.5 pounds

2. New Zealand
313.3 pounds

6. St. Lucia
273.6 pounds

8. Spain
261.5 pounds

10. French Polynesia
247.4 pounds

Taken from: Frank DeRose, "Let Them Eat Meat," *Good Magazine*, September 15, 2009, and World Resource Institute.

bowl full of flour and butterfat. I'd much rather have vegetables and grains and a few bites of chicken."

Meat Is Both Moral and Politically Correct

For Andrew and many of our ex-vegetarian friends, the ethical reasons for eating meat, combined with the health-related ones, have been impossible to deny. "The way I see it, you've got three opportunities every day to act on your values and have an immediate effect on something you're concerned about," Andrew says. "You're probably worried about Darfur[1], too, but what can you do about that every single day? Write a letter? It doesn't have the same kind of impact."

Supporting ranchers we believe in, and the stores and restaurants that sell their products, has a very tangible impact that we experience firsthand all the time. But ask most vegetarians if the battle between small, sustainable ranchers and industrial farming is at the top of their list of concerns about eating meat, and you'll probably be met with a blank stare. "For people who are against eating meat because it's wrong or offensive to eat animals, even the cleanest grass-fed beef won't be good enough," Katzen says.

Convincing those people that eating meat can improve the welfare of the entire livestock population is a tough sell. But we'll keep trying. What we've discovered is that you can hover pretty close to the bottom of the food chain and still make a difference, quietly. We've found a healthy balance somewhere between the two extremes—which, come to think of it, is also a good way to approach a marriage.

EVALUATING THE AUTHOR'S ARGUMENTS:

To make her argument, Lennon distinguishes between humanely raised, antibiotic-free meat and that which is produced and slaughtered in factory farming operations. In other words, Lennon thinks the way animals are raised and killed affects whether their consumption is moral. What do you think? Are there degrees of morality when it comes to eating meat? Is eating steak from a large-scale factory farm less moral than eating one from a local farm? Write one to two paragraphs explaining your position.

1. An area in the Sudan that has been ravaged by civil war.

Viewpoint

3

It Is Unethical to Eat Any Animal Products

Gary L. Francione

"To the extent it is morally wrong to eat flesh, it is as morally wrong—and possibly more morally wrong—to consume dairy."

In the following viewpoint, Gary L. Francione argues that consuming any animal product—even milk, eggs, or honey—is wrong. He explains that although dairy cows live longer than cows slaughtered for their meat, they are kept in equally inhumane conditions and unjustly exploited for their resources. In Francione's mind, there is no difference between killing a cow for its meat and caging it and pumping it for its milk—both actions exploit the animal and keep it from pursuing its natural lifestyle. Francione says the only way to truly respect animals is to not only refrain from eating their flesh but to avoid exploiting, enslaving, or hurting them in any way for any reason. To him, this means avoiding any animal products, and he urges vegetarians and meat eaters to do the same.

Gary L. Francione, "Vegetarianism First? The Conventional Wisdom - and Why It's Wrong," *The Vegan*, Spring 2010, pp. 12-13. Reproduced by permission.

Francione is a professor at Rutgers University School of Law in Newark, New Jersey. He also runs the web site Abolitionist Approach.com, which promotes veganism as the moral baseline of the animal rights movement.

AS YOU READ, CONSIDER THE FOLLOWING QUESTIONS:
1. What does the author say is similar to promoting the eating of cows with spots rather than cows without spots? What does he mean by this?
2. In what way are cage-free eggs and organic milk "gimmicks", according to Francione?
3. Who is Donald Watson and how does he factor into the author's argument?

"Discussing veganism with people who are omnivores is too difficult. You have to start with vegetarianism."

Every vegan has heard this notion expressed many, many times; indeed, it passes for conventional wisdom among those of us who take animal ethics seriously.

I would like to suggest that the conventional wisdom on this matter is wrong and that we should educate everyone, including and particularly omnivores, about veganism and should never promote vegetarianism as morally preferable to being an omnivore.

There Is No Moral Distinction Between Meat and Dairy

There is no morally significant distinction between flesh and other animal products. Animals used in dairy are generally kept alive longer than those used for meat, are treated every bit as badly if not worse, and end up in the same slaughterhouse. Moreover, the slaughter of animals for meat and the dairy industry are inextricably intertwined in that there would be no veal industry without the dairy industry and dairy cows are all slaughtered and consumed.

I have said many times that if I were forced to choose between eating a steak or drinking milk and I was to make the decision solely on the basis of suffering, I would choose the steak. To promote vegetarianism rather than veganism is similar to—and as nonsensical as—promoting eating the meat from spotted cows rather than the meat from cows without spots.

When we promote this artificial distinction, it is even more difficult for someone who gives up flesh to go vegan because she sees no reason to. As often as I have heard animal advocates urge that we should promote vegetarianism rather than veganism, I have heard vegans say that they remained vegetarians for many years before going vegan because they believed that they were being "compassionate" and acting morally, and were discharging their moral obligations to animals by not eating flesh but eating dairy products.

We should never present flesh as somehow morally distinguishable from dairy. To the extent it is morally wrong to eat flesh, it is as morally wrong—and possibly more morally wrong—to consume dairy.

How Do We Raise the Issue of Veganism?

Animal advocates often ask me: how do we raise the issue of veganism with omnivores without having them turn us off at the outset?

It's easier than you think. As a general matter, it is almost always easier to have a discussion with someone if that person does not feel that you are judging her in a negative way and if you engage the thinking processes of the other person.

So it is always preferable to discuss the matter of veganism in a non-judgmental way. Remember that to most people, eating flesh or dairy and using animal products

> **FAST FACT**
>
> Surveys by *Time* magazine and *Vegetarian Journal* have shown that vegans compose somewhere between 0.2 percent and 1.3 percent of the U.S. population.

such as leather, wool, and silk, is as normal as breathing air or drinking water. A person who consumes dairy or uses animal products is not necessarily or usually what a recent and unpopular American president labeled an "evil doer."

The most effective way to get someone to "get" veganism is to demonstrate how it fits with what she already believes. You can do

A Life Without Animal Products

Vegans avoid all food and material goods that are either made directly from animals or require the suffering of animals in their creation. This means they avoid:

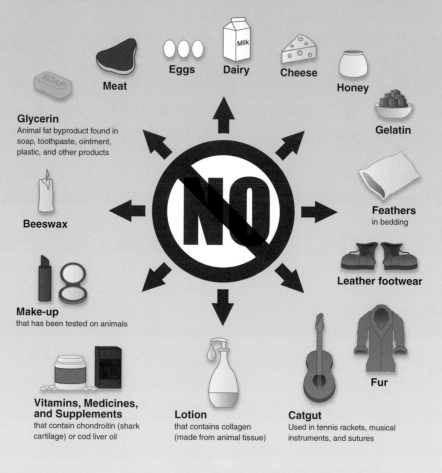

Meat

Eggs

Dairy

Cheese

Honey

Glycerin
Animal fat byproduct found in soap, toothpaste, ointment, plastic, and other products

Gelatin

Beeswax

Feathers
in bedding

Make-up
that has been tested on animals

Leather footwear

Fur

Vitamins, Medicines, and Supplements
that contain chondroitin (shark cartilage) or cod liver oil

Lotion
that contains collagen (made from animal tissue)

Catgut
Used in tennis rackets, musical instruments, and sutures

Compiled by editor.

this in a number of ways. Here's an actual example of an exchange, lightly edited, that I had recently on a live chat program:

"Do you agree with the notion that it is wrong to inflict unnecessary suffering or death on animals?"

"Yes, of course."

"We could have an interesting discussion about the fine points of "necessity," but would you agree that it is wrong to inflict suffering and death on animals for reasons of pleasure, amusement, or convenience?"

"No brainer. Sure. I really objected when it was revealed that [American football player] Michael Vick was involved with fighting dogs. I think it's barbaric to do that."

"Why?"

"It's obvious. It's wrong to make animals suffer and die for our amusement."

"Do you eat meat or cheese or drink milk?"

"Yes, I do not eat much beef because I know it's bad for you but I eat pork, chicken, and fish. And I love cheese and ice cream."

"What is the difference between what you're doing and what Michael Vick did?"

"What? I don't understand."

"Well, Michael Vick imposed suffering and death on animals because he enjoyed the results. Those of us who eat meat and dairy impose suffering and death on animals because we enjoy the results.

We just pay someone else to do the dirty work."

"But surely there's a difference."

"What is that difference? You don't need to eat animal products. Indeed, many mainstream health care professionals agree that animal products are detrimental to human health. And animal agriculture is unquestionably an ecological nightmare. The best justification that we have for inflicting pain, suffering, and death on more than 56 billion animals annually, not counting fish, is that they taste good."

"I never thought of it like that."

We had another follow-up chat about the treatment of cows in the production of dairy. Three days later, the person involved in this exchange wrote to tell me that she had decided to become vegan.

Veganism: Incremental Steps

I am often asked what to say to a person who expresses agreement with the moral theory of veganism but says that she cannot go vegan right away.

First of all, I always emphasize that it is easy to go vegan. I very consciously reject the notion promoted by many animal advocates that veganism is difficult. It's easy. I have been a vegan for 27 years

Many animal rights advocates believe that slaughtering cows and keeping them penned-up in factory dairy farms is unethical.

now. It was more difficult when I started but it was not that difficult, even in 1982. In 2009, it's a breeze. And if you want to eat healthily and avoid prepared foods, it's even easier.

Second, I *never* encourage anyone to eat cage-free eggs or "happy meat" or organic milk, etc. First of all, all of these animals are tortured. Although animals who are supposedly raised in "free-range" circumstances, or whose products are advertised as "organic," are raised in conditions that *may* be *slightly* less brutal than the normal factory farm, they are all still tortured. I will never portray these products as anything but what they are: gimmicks that are intended to make humans feel more comfortable about consuming nonhumans.

Third, I encourage those who really are unwilling to go vegan immediately to follow the "Vegan 1-2-3" plan. This introduces veganism in three stages. The person goes vegan for breakfast for some period of time (a few weeks, a month). She sees how easy it is and how delicious and satisfying a vegan breakfast is. She then goes vegan for lunch for some period of time, and then for dinner, and then she's vegan.

Although I think that the Vegan 1-2-3 plan is preferable to eating "happy" meat or dairy, I never concede that eating animal products is ever morally right. I always want to be clear that veganism is the only position that makes sense if you take animal interests seriously. The other person is always clear that even if she is not ready to go vegan immediately, nothing short of veganism will discharge the important moral obligation involved.

We Should Completely Eliminate Animal Products from Our Lives

Donald Watson, who founded The Vegan Society in 1944 and who lived a healthy, active life until passing on in 2005, maintained that dairy products, such as milk, eggs, and cheese, were every bit as cruel and exploitive of sentient animal life as was slaughtering animals for their flesh: "The unquestionable cruelty associated with the production of dairy produce has made it clear that lacto-vegetarianism is but a half-way house between flesh-eating and a truly humane, civilised diet, and we think, therefore, that during our life on earth we should try to evolve sufficiently to make the 'full journey.'" He also avoided wearing leather, wool or silk and used a fork, rather than a spade in his gardening to avoid killing worms.

Let us instill in others the reverence for life that Donald Watson had and that he passed on to us.

EVALUATING THE AUTHOR'S ARGUMENTS:

To make his argument, Francione imagines a conversation he would have with a vegetarian to convince him or her that in addition to meat, consuming milk, eggs, and other animal products is wrong. If you were the person he was talking to, would you be convinced? Why or why not?

An Animal Product–Free Diet Is Unhealthy and Impractical

Natasha Mann

"With a vegan diet you are really making a difficult job for yourself. It is absolutely not something that should be tried without support from a dietician."

Natasha Mann is a reporter for the London newspaper *The Independent*. In the following viewpoint, she reports on a family whose health suffered after following a strict vegan diet in which they avoided all animal products, including milk, butter, eggs, and honey. Eating this way left Holly Paige and her children deficient in critical vitamins and proteins, which led to serious health problems. Paige argues she and her children became healthier and had more energy once they started consuming milk, eggs, and fish. Mann concludes it is very difficult to be a healthy vegan—without the support of a nutritionist, most people, especially children, get sick or fail to thrive.

One morning over breakfast, Holly Paige looked at her daughter and realised things weren't right. Lizzie should have been flourishing. Instead, her cheeks were pinched, she was small for her age, and although she had skinny arms and legs, her belly was big and swollen. When Lizzie smiled, Paige suddenly noticed her upper front teeth were pitted with holes.

"I was absolutely horrified," recalls Paige.

A Dangerous Diet

At the time, Paige was feeding them what she thought was the most nutritious diet possible. They had been raw vegans for three years, and ate plenty of fruit, vegetables, nuts, seeds, grains, soya and pulses, but no meat, fish or dairy. According to the raw-food doctrine, Lizzie and Bertie, then three and four-and-a-half, should have been brimming with good health. But Paige's mothering instinct was on the alert.

"I knew something was wrong, but I couldn't put a finger on it," says Paige, 45. "They were two sizes behind in clothes. Of course, children come in all different shapes and sizes, but their growth seemed to be slowing further. I have two older children so I had their development to measure Lizzie and Bertie's against."

There were other oddities: "I remember going to the supermarket and buying butter for my older children. Lizzie, who had never had butter in her life, would grab the packet and gnaw into it," says Paige. "It was really disconcerting. I would be thinking, 'What is going on? Here is this purely fed child—why would she need to do this?' I was so brainwashed into thinking dairy products are bad for you."

Vegans Are a Very Small Minority

The overwhelming majority of Americans eat meat, fish, or dairy. Just a small percentage identify themselves as vegetarian, and an even smaller number are vegan (meaning they consume or use no animal products).

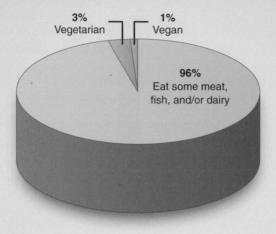

3%
Vegetarian

1%
Vegan

96%
Eat some meat, fish, and/or dairy

Taken from: Vegetarian Resource Group and Harris Interactive, Inc. poll, May 1–5, 2009.

"It Felt Wrong"

When she took Lizzie and Bertie to her health visitor, she didn't seem too concerned. "She said they were in the low percentile, but thought they were OK," says Paige. "Yet I knew the children weren't growing. I could sense that there was something wrong. It felt wrong."

Finally, Paige stumbled across the answer in an old vitamin book. Although she has no medical confirmation, she believes the family had symptoms of vitamin D- and protein-deficiency. "I felt like such an idiot. I got the information from a book I'd had sitting around on my shelf for 20 years."

The discovery brought a swift end to her experience of veganism. In Totnes [England], where she lives, Paige knows many other raw vegans who have a nature-loving lifestyle. But despite taking a daily supplement that included vitamin D and B12, she and the children were suffering. Today, the family still mainly has a raw diet, but Paige includes butter, cheese, eggs and occasionally fish. "I had let malnutrition in through the back door in the name of health," says Paige. "It was ridiculous."

Vegan Diets Can Contribute to Disease

There is a significant difference between being vegan (and eating cooked foods) and raw vegan. Vegans benefit from fortified cereals, baked goods and a wider variety of grains and pulses; what's more, cooking aids the absorption of some micronutrients. But Lisa Miles, from the British Nutrition Foundation, says: "The most dramatic change to the diet is being vegan rather than the raw element, because you are cutting out two huge food groups. This affects vitamin D and protein."

Last week, strict diets for children were questioned after a 12-year-old vegan girl was admitted to a Scottish hospital with rickets. Her spine was said to resemble that of an 80-year-old woman.

> **FAST FACT**
>
> According to *New York Times* reporter Nina Planck, a vegan diet may lack vitamins B12, A, and D, which are found in meat, fish, eggs and butter, and necessary minerals such as zinc and calcium.

Rickets is a degenerative bone condition that can lead to curvature of the spine and bone fractures. It is caused by a lack of vitamin D, usually found in oily fish, eggs, butter and made by our bodies from sunshine—although in the UK the sun is only strong enough to do this between April and September. It's a disease you might more commonly associate with the Dickensian character, Tiny Tim.

Many dieticians believe it is possible to bring up a healthy vegan child. "You can do it, but you do have to make sure you know what you are doing, especially in regards to weight," says Jackie Lowdon from the British Dietician Association. "As with any self-restricting diet, you need to get proper professional advice."

Vegan Diets Make It Harder to Be Healthy

The Vegan Society, unsurprisingly, claim that the diet is suitable for all stages of life, and have an army of strapping, healthy adults brought up as vegans from birth who are happy to talk to the media. They also publish a book with dietary advice on feeding vegan children, written by dietician Sandra Hood. A spokeswoman, however, says they would not recommend a raw vegan diet for children.

Nigel Denby, a dietician and author of *Nutrition for Dummies*, says: "It can be hard enough bringing a child up to eat healthily, but with a vegan diet you are really making a difficult job for yourself. It is absolutely not something that should be tried without support from a dietician."

Several factors, says Denby, make a vegan diet for small children more difficult. With a restricted range of foods, if children turn their

A vegan diet may not be healthy for children unless their essential vitamins and nutrients are carefully monitored.

nose up at one particular food, you could be stuck for choice. "With smaller appetites and portion sizes, children under five have higher nutrient requirements than adults. Therefore, every mealtime has to be an opportunity to feed them high-nutrient-based foods."

Care must be taken with certain nutrients. "Haem iron, found in meat, is easier for the body to absorb," explains Denby. "Non-haem iron, which is just as good, is found in leafy vegetables and fortified cereals, but you have to eat a greater amount to get the same amount of iron."

A Need for Meat and Dairy

Paige now believes that her children were craving dairy products. "It was confusing because for the first year I felt good, calm and content, and had plenty of energy. The children didn't have childhood sicknesses. But something seemed to be missing. We were always picking between meals, always obsessed by food."

Paige believes long-term breastfeeding helped sustain Lizzie and Bertie, but the toll of veganism on her own health was dramatic: "It was the third year when my body started disintegrating, frighteningly fast. I was getting thin, losing muscle and I was going to bed at half nine." She would also have "mad" binges, and eat nothing but rice cakes and butter.

The last straw came when Paige's eldest son Bruce came to stay. He asked her to buy chicken, and Paige ended up eating half of it. After that, she couldn't stop. "I just went wild. Typically, in a day I would eat half a chicken, two litres of milk, half a pound of cheese and three eggs. I just had to do it. It went on for weeks. The children were having lots of boiled eggs and cheese."

Paige, who now runs an online magazine and raw food shop, says her biggest lesson is never to be too restrictive again. "For a lot of people, there is something about these various nutrients in the animal form that we can assimilate. I don't know why, but experience shows a lot of us can't get enough protein on a vegan diet."

Finally Thriving

Now when Paige looks at her two youngest, now seven and eight she is certain they are thriving. "There was a moment when I was worried damage had been done for life," she says. "Now, I'm confident they are doing well. Even though they eat as much fruit and dried fruit as before, their teeth haven't had one bit more decay."

And nowadays, it's their growth that's the big talking point. "The first thing anyone says when they visit is: 'My, haven't they grown?'"

EVALUATING THE AUTHORS' ARGUMENTS:

This viewpoint used the Paige family's story to argue that it is unhealthy to eat a diet devoid of animal products. What do you think Gary L. Francione, author of the previous viewpoint, would say about the problems the Paige family encountered while eating vegan? After reading both viewpoints, what is your opinion about veganism—is it healthy? Is it more moral than other diets? Why or why not?

Chapter 3

Should Animals Be Used in Scientific Experiments?

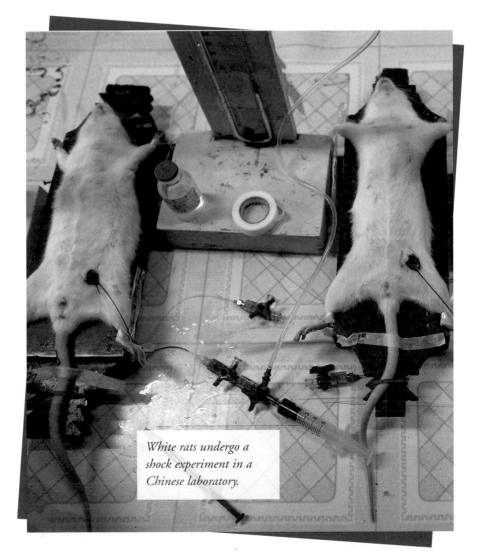

White rats undergo a shock experiment in a Chinese laboratory.

Animal Experimentation Is Necessary

George Poste

> *"Animal studies continue to be necessary for advancing human and animal health and have played a vital role in virtually every major medical advance."*

George Poste is a veterinarian and director of the Biodesign Institute at Arizona State University. In the following viewpoint he explains why he believes animal testing is necessary. He says using animals is the only way researchers can develop effective drugs, vaccines, and other life-saving medicines. In his opinion, just because research involves animals does not mean it is necessarily unethical. The animals are not harmed more than necessary or tested on for fun or curiosity's sake. Furthermore, researchers only test on animals because they produce the most reliable data—in fact, says Poste, scientists would replace animals if they could because tests involving them are expensive and time-consuming. But since an accurate non-animal alternative does not yet exist for high-level medical tests, Poste concludes that animal research is needed to develop the medicines and products humans need.

AS YOU READ, CONSIDER THE FOLLOWING QUESTIONS:
1. What discomfort does Poste say animal rights activists prey on?
2. Name at least four items Poste says would not be possible without animal testing.
3. How does the author characterize tactics used by animal rights groups against the company Covance?

A s a veterinarian and someone who has spent three decades in biomedical research in academia and the pharmaceutical industry, I know that animal research saves lives.

With the announcement of [pharmaceutical company] Covance's plans for a major drug development facility in Chandler [Arizona], I am concerned by deceptive claims from extremist groups about the need for animal research.

Vital for Medicine and Research

Animal studies continue to be necessary for advancing human and animal health and have played a vital role in virtually every major medical advance. This includes lifesaving drugs and vaccines, new surgical procedures and improved diagnosis of disease.

A hallmark of humanity is our ability to care about other species. It is understandably difficult for people to reconcile this empathy with support of animal studies for medical advances that cure disease and improve the quality of life.

Animal extremists prey on this discomfort and count on society's general lack of scientific insight to advance their agenda. These extremists knowingly misrepresent the ability of computers and emerging scientific techniques to serve as viable substitutes for animal studies.

No Replacement Yet for Animals in Research

Government regulations around the world require that new drugs, vaccines and surgical implants first be tested in animals for potential toxic reactions. Beyond these formal legal requirements, research into the root causes of disease at the genetic level and how diseases become resistant to current treatments cannot be simulated by computer programs or duplicated in test tubes.

American Opinions of Animal Testing

The majority of Americans approve of using animals in experiments, though slightly more Americans are likely to approve of such testing if it is done for medical research rather than the development of products.

Do you support or oppose banning all *product* testing on animals?

39%
Strongly or somewhat support banning product testing

2%
Unsure

59%
Strongly or somewhat oppose banning product testing

Do you support or oppose banning all *medical research* on laboratory animals?

35%
Strongly or somewhat support banning medical research

1%
Unsure

64%
Strongly or somewhat oppose banning medical research

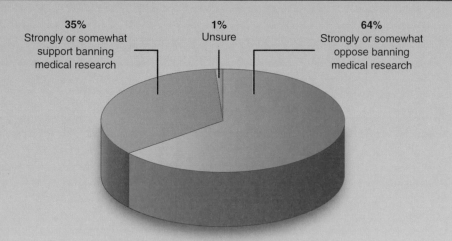

Taken from: Gallup poll, May 8–11, 2008.

Although present-day technology cannot yet replace many types of animal research, the research community is committed to finding new ways to reduce and replace animal testing. This ethical commitment is embodied in strict animal welfare protocols at most university, government and industrial laboratories.

In addition to humane considerations, the economic and logistical advantages of replacing animal testing are compelling. Animal studies are time-consuming and resource-intensive. If meaningful alternatives existed, companies could save hundreds of millions of dollars in facilities and personnel costs.

A Life Without Animal Testing Is Unrealistic

Opposition to all animal testing would require a life without drugs, vaccines, painkillers, anesthetics and surgery. It would demand a rejection of all federally mandated Food and Drug Administration and Environmental Protection Agency tests that ensure the safe consumption of products in our homes and workplaces, ranging from the testing of components used in computers and cellphones to plastic wraps and chemical additives in our foods and drinks. In short, it would require a lifestyle far removed from that enjoyed by most people, particularly the jet-setting celebrities who oppose animal research.

> # FAST FACT
>
> Animal research falls under three broad categories: pure research, applied research, and toxicology. Pure research is undirected research that does not have an immediately applicable goal. Applied research has a specific goal, such as a treatment for a particular disease. Toxicology research uses animals to test substances, such as pharmaceuticals, for toxic effects they might have in humans.

Research on Animals Can Be Ethical

Reducing complex issues to oversimplified sound bites encourages the thinking that wearing a lapel ribbon is a substitute for education and dedication to seeking solutions. Research scientists, physicians and veterinarians face tough moral and ethical issues in this pursuit and take these responsibilities seriously.

Concern about animal welfare can take very different forms. Some people are offended by the use of leather and fur as fashion accessories but accept that medical research must unavoidably use animals until viable alternatives are found. Some groups argue persuasively against intensive farming practices but, again, recognize the need for animals in medical research. I recently signed a petition in Arizona calling for reform in the raising of veal calves.

The even-tempered beagle is widely used for toxicity tests, surgery research, and dental experiments. Without animal testing there would be far fewer drugs, vaccines, painkillers, anesthetics, and surgeries available.

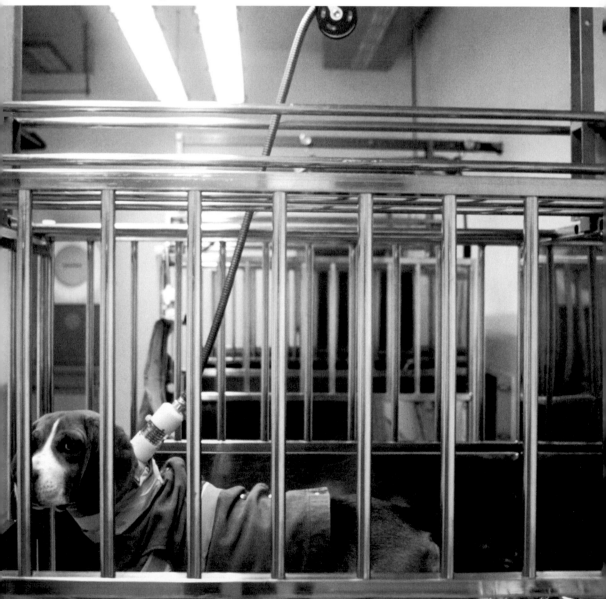

Animal Rights Groups Cannot Be Trusted

My advice is that people carefully consider not just whether or not a group shares their beliefs, but whether or not they behave in an ethical manner. The tactics used by opponents of Covance in Chandler have included false claims about alternatives to animal testing and misinformation aimed at provoking community concerns about potential disasters.

Well-funded national groups often disguise their involvement to make it appear as if local citizens are leading the effort. In May [2006], *The Arizona Republic* uncovered deceptive methods and use of false names by a leading opponent of the Chandler drug-development facility in an attempt to camouflage ties to People for the Ethical Treatment of Animals and involvement in other protest campaigns.

Animal Rights Activists Are Dangerous

Of greatest concern are those who encourage violence in the name of animal activism. My family and I have been the targets of death threats, as have many of my colleagues. Several animal extremist organizations have been identified by the FBI as serious domestic terrorism threats.

People for the Ethical Treatment of Animals provides funding to the Animal Liberation Front, which is listed as a terrorist group by the governments of both the United States and the United Kingdom.

A publicly available report from the FBI describes People for the Ethical Treatment of Animals as an organization that "recruits interns for the sole purpose of committing criminal acts."

In 2003, a representative of the Physicians Committee for Responsible Medicine, another national group that has been prominent in the local debate, called for the assassination of doctors whose research involves animals.

Americans Support the Need for Animal Research

Fortunately, very few people endorse such extreme views. Surveys show that most Americans support the need for animal studies aimed at medical advances. Even as divergent as the views of animal activists and researchers may seem to be, there is agreement on one key issue: We all look forward to a day when mankind's ingenuity provides a way to completely eliminate the need for animal studies.

I have a challenge to offer to anyone who feels strongly about this topic, especially young people. If you sincerely wish to eliminate the need for animal research, put down your picket signs, learn about the subject and invent solutions. I guarantee you'll find a receptive audience in the medical research community, because it's a goal we share.

EVALUATING THE AUTHOR'S ARGUMENTS:

Poste is a veterinarian, someone committed to healing and treating animals. Does knowing this about his background influence your opinion of his argument? If so, in what way? Are you surprised that a veterinarian would support animal testing? Why or why not?

Viewpoint 2

Animal Experimentation Is Not Necessary

Peter Tatchell

"What applies to mice, dogs, monkeys or rabbits may not necessarily apply to humans. Our physiology is sufficiently different to invalidate most cures devised by animal experimentation."

In the following viewpoint, Peter Tatchell argues it is not necessary to use animals for research. He says that many scientific tests on animals do not produce data that is applicable to humans. For example, tests that study how the human immunodeficiency virus (HIV) works in animals produce results that are applicable only to the test animals, but not to humans. In Tatchell's opinion, using animals for these tests produces useless data because the tests will have to be re-run on people anyway. For tests that do provide data that is useful for humans, Tatchell says non-animal alternatives exist that provide accurate, reliable results and spare animals harm and suffering in the process. For all of these reasons, Tatchell concludes that using animals for scientific research is an outdated and unnecessary activity. Unfortunately, says Tatchell, non-animal testing alternatives are underfunded and need more public and government support in order to become widespread.

Tatchell is a British human and animal rights activist. He contributes regularly to the *Guardian* newspaper, where this viewpoint was originally published.

AS YOU READ, CONSIDER THE FOLLOWING QUESTIONS:
1. How many medical experiments on animals took place in Great Britain in 2008, according to Tatchell?
2. What are macaques, and what problem does Tatchell have with using them for research?
3. What is the Dr. Hadwen Trust and how does it support the author's argument?

The government has been assuring us for many years that animal experiments are only sanctioned for high priority medical research, as a last resort. We were told that the trend was for fewer laboratory procedures using animals. Indeed, the government boasted that it was committed to big cuts in animal-based research through the development of replacement methods. This seemed to be the case for several years, when the use of lab animals steadily declined.

It therefore comes as a major surprise to learn that in 2008 the number of medical experiments involving animals has shown the largest rise since modern records began. Home Office figures state that nearly 3.7 million experiments were performed on animals last year, a rise of 454,000 or 14% on the previous year. This is the steepest increase in animal use in medical research since 1986, when the government introduced new recording and monitoring procedures.

Animals Share Many Qualities with Humans

While most experiments in 2008 involved mice, macaque monkeys were used in 1,000 extra experiments, a hike of 33%. This trend is particularly disturbing and difficult to justify, given that macaques (and other monkeys used in UK labs) are intelligent, social animals. They share many human-like attributes, including language, tool-use, reasoning, emotions, improvisation, planning, empathy and the capacity to feel both physical and psychological pain. The mere fact of their imprisonment in laboratory cages—usually in solitary confinement—is a serious abuse of these thinking, feeling creatures.

The spike in animal experimentation coincides with the 50th anniversary of landmark proposals to find alternatives. Alas, for half a century successive governments have failed to fund the promised development of replacement methods—even though every scientist knows that animal models are flawed and imperfect approximations of the human body and human disease.

Over a decade ago, I was invited to join a working party based at the Medical Research Council's head office in London. The aim was to look at ways of replacing animal research with credible, rigorous humane options. But in the end, despite the shiny promises, neither the MRC nor the government was willing to stump up the money to devise cruelty-free alternatives. The meetings were all talk and PR spin. I walked out in despair.

The recent jump in animal research has been condemned by animal rights campaigners who have

called for a new co-ordinated effort to reduce the number of animals used in medical research. "With the scientific expertise this country has to offer we should have seen far greater progress to replace animals with more advanced techniques," said Sebastien Farnaud of the Dr Hadwen Trust for Humane Research. The organisation called on political parties to agree to a "roadmap to replacement" to reduce the use of animals in research.

Alternatives to Animal Subjects Are Possible

Replacement of animals is possible in many spheres of medical research. Remember how the supporters of vivisection [animal testing] used to say that it was impossible and dangerous to halt the animal testing of cosmetics and household products? Well, despite their scaremongering, it has been possible to safely replace many animal tests that were previously said to be "irreplaceable." The Dr Hadwen Trust

ANIMAL TESTING

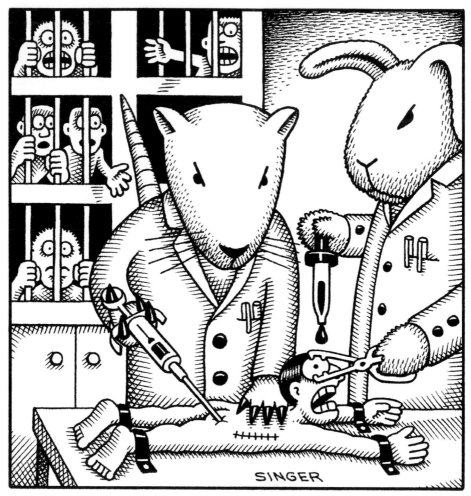

has shown that alternatives are safe and effective. With tiny amounts of self-generated funding, it has already financed the development of successful, scientifically-validated alternatives to experiments that were once conducted with animals, including brain, kidney, diabetes and rheumatism research.

Non-Animal Experimentation Has Much to Offer

Of course, some animal research has provided breakthroughs in medical science. But these breakthroughs might have also come about through non-animal experimentation if they had been equally well funded. There is also a problem with information gleaned from animals in labs. What applies to mice, dogs, monkeys or rabbits may not necessarily apply to humans. Our physiology is sufficiently different to invalidate most cures devised by animal experimentation.

HIV, for example, is deadly to humans but not to most laboratory animals. So studying HIV in other species may not produce results that are applicable to humans. The same goes for any treatments devised for HIV. They may work in chimpanzees or cats, but not in people. Animal research is often bad science. Human-centred research invariably gets more accurate, effective and safe results. "The animals provide data—of course they do—but it's the wrong data," said Andre Menache from Animal Aid. "It applies to monkeys; it doesn't apply to people.

"Whatever you discover, you will have to re-discover using people, so not only do the animals suffer using these experiments, the first few patients using these novel treatments will suffer, too. In fact, there are 700 treatments for stroke that work in laboratory animals—only one works in people and even that one treatment is controversial. We are doing something wrong," he told BBC News.

Activist Peter Tatchell believes that animal testing can be eliminated because there is enough non-animal testing that provides accurate and reliable results.

Animal Research: A Blot on Humanity

For me, cruelty is barbarism, whether it is inflicted on humans or on other species. The campaigns for animal rights and human rights share the same fundamental aim: a kinder, gentler world without oppression and suffering, based on care and compassion. The abuse of animals in farming, sport, circuses, zoos, the fashion industry and medical experiments is a blot on humanity. The sooner we end it, the better.

EVALUATING THE AUTHORS' ARGUMENTS:

Tatchell says it is no longer necessary to use animals for scientific research since alternative, non-animal based research methods can be used to run accurate, reliable tests. How would George Poste, author of the previous viewpoint, respond to this claim? After reading both viewpoints, which author do you think is right, and why?

It Is Ethical to Use Animals for Medical Testing If It Saves Human Lives

Robert Winston and John Illman

"Medical research with animals has helped to extend and improve the quality of life for millions of people."

In the following viewpoint, Robert Winston and John Illman argue that animals remain a vital part of conducting accurate, life-saving medical research. They explore ten ways in which medical testing on animals has resulted in cures, drugs, or other developments that have allowed millions of sick people to be healthier or more comfortable. They say that when scientists involve animals in their research, they do so with care, humility, and humanity, never testing unnecessarily or arbitrarily harming an animal. Furthermore, when non-animal testing alternatives are available, they use them if doing so will produce reliable, accurate data. Winston and Illman conclude that because animal testing has been a critical factor in improving the lives of millions of people, it is ethical and should be continued.

Winston (a professor) and Illman (a medical journalist) are associated with Pro-Test, a UK-based group that promotes and supports scientific research that involves animal testing.

AS YOU READ, CONSIDER THE FOLLOWING QUESTIONS:
1. What do the authors say was the finding of a 2006 Royal Society report?
2. How has testing on animals impacted breast cancer research? What about Parkinson's disease research?
3. What percentage of medical research do the authors say is done without animals?

Scientific and medical research is a drawn-out process and the contribution of animal research is frequently overlooked by the time successful therapy reaches patients. We live longer and healthier lives than ever before.

Animal Testing Has Improved Human Health
Whilst there have been remarkable improvements in the human environment, animal research has played a major part in developing improvements in human health. Animal research advanced the treatment of infections, helped with immunisation, improved cancer treatment and has had a major impact on managing heart disease, brain disorders, arthritis and transplantation. My own field, the prevention of genetic disorders in babies, was possible only because of humane work on animals.

Animal research contributed to 70% of the Nobel prizes for physiology or medicine. Many award-winning scientists affirm that they could not have made their discoveries without animals. Polio would still claim hundreds of lives annually in Britain without the animal research of the Nobel laureate Albert Sabin. "There could have been no oral polio vaccine without the use of innumerable animals," he once said. Animals are still needed to test every new batch of polio vaccine produced for today's children.

Research on Animals Is Performed with Care

The work we do is performed with compassion, care, humanity and humility. All my rabbits, when I worked with them years ago, were stroked and petted every day. Their contribution changed the understanding of ectopic pregnancy—the commonest cause of maternal death worldwide. My genetically modified rodents breed happily, and their offspring are indistinguishable from those of other rats and mice. Medical researchers are compassionate people seeking to alleviate pain and suffering. They are unlikely to do anything that is unnecessary or cruel. Indeed, they are not allowed to, because of the rigour with which animal licences are granted by government.

Alternatives to Animals Don't Work

Animal research is not done in isolation; it is one vital strand of medical research. Of course, there are differences between animals and people. But there are also striking similarities, meaning animals provide invaluable information—information that cannot be replaced by computer modelling, cell culture or human experimentation. Mice have virtually the same genes as humans, which is why they are so useful for understanding human physiology and disease. And it is important to remember that animal research plays a vital role in understanding animal ill-health, as well.

For honest, open debate we need to understand the role of research using animals in medical progress.

> **FAST FACT**
>
> According to the group Understanding Animal Research, medical testing on animals has helped develop treatments or cures for multiple types of cancer, HIV and AIDS, high blood pressure, asthma, blood diseases, organ transplants, meningitis, Parkinson's disease, and many other diseases and disorders.

. . . Tracing the research process—from 'blue-sky' or chance observation, through careful studies which include the use of animals for the ultimate benefit of people who are ill—will increase understanding of this essential endeavour.

Over a Century of Medical Discoveries

Animal testing has led to some of the most important medical discoveries of the modern age. What follows is a timeline of such breakthroughs—the animals that were tested on are listed in parentheses.

Pre-20th Century
Malaria parasite lifecycle (cattle, birds)
Vaccine for smallpox (cattle)
Vaccine for anthrax (sheep)
Early anaesthetics (cats, rabbits, dogs)
Rabies vaccine (rabbits, dogs)
Typhoid, cholera, and plague vaccines (mice, rats)
Treatment for beriberi (chickens)

1900s
Treatment for rickets (dogs)
Corneal transplants (rabbits)
Local anaesthetics (rabbits, dogs)
Discovery of Vitamin C (guinea pigs)

1910s
Blood transfusions (dogs, guinea pigs, rabbits)

1920s
Insulin (dogs, rabbits, mice)
Canine distemper vaccine (dogs)

1930s
Modern anaesthetics (rats, rabbits, dogs, cats, monkeys)
Tetanus vaccine (horses, guinea pigs)
Diphtheria vaccine (guinea pigs, rabbits, horses, monkeys)
Anticoagulants (rabbits, guinea pigs, mice, dogs)

1940s
Penicillin and streptomycin (mice)
Discovery of rhesus factor (monkeys)
Kidney dialysis (guinea pigs, rabbits, dogs, monkeys)
Whooping cough vaccine (mice, rabbits)
Heart-lung machine for open heart surgery (dogs)

1950s
Polio vaccine (mice, monkeys)
Hip replacement surgery (dogs, sheep, goats)
Kidney transplants (dogs)
Cardiac pacemakers (dogs)
Medicines for high blood pressure (rats, mice, dogs)
Replacement heart valves (dogs, calves, rabbits, guinea pigs, rats)
Chlorpromazine and other psychiatric medicines (rats, rabbits, monkeys)

1960s
Heart transplants (dogs)
Coronary bypass operations (dogs)
German measles vaccine (monkeys)
MMR vaccine (monkeys)
Antidepressants and antipsychotics (rats, guinea pigs, rabbits)

1970s
CT scanning for improved diagnosis (pigs)
Chemotherapy for leukaemia (mice)
Medicines to treat ulcers (rats, dogs)
Inhaled asthma medication (guinea pigs, rabbits)

1980s
MRI scanning for improved diagnosis (rabbits, pigs)
Prenatal corticosteroids improving survival of premature babies (sheep, rabbits, cattle)
Treatment for river blindness (rodents, cattle)
Life support systems for premature babies (monkeys)
Medicines to control transplant rejection (mice, rabbits, dogs, monkeys)
Hepatitis B vaccines (monkeys)
Medicines to treat viral diseases (many species)
Treatment for leprosy (armadillos, monkeys)

1990s
Combined therapy for HIV infection (mice, monkeys)
Meningitis vaccines (mice)
Better medicines for depression (rats)
Medicines for breast and prostate cancer (mice, rats, dogs)
Medicines for type 2 diabetes (mice)
New medicines for asthma (guinea pigs, monkeys)
Statins to lower cholesterol (rabbits)

2000s
Deep Brain Stimulation for Parkinson's Disease (monkeys)
Monoclonal antibodies for adult leukaemia, lymphoma (mice)
Cervical cancer vaccine (rabbits, cattle)
Clotting agent from milk (goats)
Bird flu vaccine (chickens, ferrets)

2010s
Stem cells for spinal cord, heart repair (mice, rats)
Oral or inhaled insulin for type 1 diabetes (mice)
Angiogenesis inhibitors for cancer, blindness (mice)
Gene therapy for muscular dystrophy, cystic fibrosis, sickle cell disease (mice)
Alzheimer's vaccine (mice)
Malaria vaccine (mice, monkeys)

Taken from: "Medical Advances and Animal Research: The Contribution of Animal Science to the Medical Revolution; Some Case Histories," Understanding Animal Research in Medicine and Coalition for Medical Progress, 2007.

Ten Medical Advances That Changed the World

Throughout the world people enjoy a better quality of life because of advances made possible through medical research, and the development of new medicines and treatments. A small but vital part of that work involves the use of animals.

Mainstream medical and scientific organisations all agree that animal research is essential for medical progress. For example, a Royal Society report stated in 2006 that: "We have all benefited immensely from scientific research involving animals. From antibiotics and insulin to blood transfusions and treatments for cancer or HIV, virtually every medical achievement in the past century has depended directly or indirectly on research on animals."

The following are examples of these achievements:

Penicillin Florey and Chain first tested the effects of penicillin in mice in 1940. By 1941, penicillin was being used to treat dying soldiers. This research won the Nobel Prize in 1945.

Blood transfusion Blood transfusion has saved the lives of countless people and animals. The technique was developed when citrated blood was shown to be safe for transfusion in dogs in 1914.

First Medicine For Tuberculosis A hundred years ago, tuberculosis (TB) was one of the most common causes of death. Nobel–Prize-winning research on guinea pigs in the 1940s led to the antibiotic streptomycin.

Meningitis Vaccine Vaccines for meningitis were developed in mice and have resulted in a huge fall in the disease. Previously many victims died or had amputations or organ damage.

Kidney Transplants Of the 5,000 people who develop kidney failure every year in the UK, one in three would die without a kidney transplant. Transplantation techniques were developed using dogs and pigs.

Breast Cancer Breast cancer is the commonest cancer among women. Animal studies led to the development of tamoxifen, one of the most successful treatments, and more recently Herceptin and aromatase inhibitors.

Asthma Inhalers Asthma is the commonest serious childhood illness and still causes about 2,000 deaths a year in the UK. Animal research was vital for the medicines in the inhalers seen in many schools today.

Polio Vaccine This advance alone has saved millions of lives. Forty years of research using monkeys and mice led to the introduction of the vaccine in the 1950s.

Insulin For Diabetes Banting and Best won the 1923 Nobel Prize for the discovery of insulin in dogs. This has saved millions of lives.

Implants For Parkinson's Disease Research carried out on experimental animals, including primates, has led to an electrical implant (similar to a heart pacemaker) for the treatment of Parkinson's Disease.

Millions of People Have Benefited

Medical research with animals has helped to extend and improve the quality of life for millions of people. It has had an equally far-reaching effect on pets and farm animals. . . .

As a medical journalist for more than 30 years, I know about the critical role of animal research, and as an individual I have good reason for being grateful. I almost certainly owe my life to animal research. The emergency operation that saved my life in 1994 was based on techniques developed through animal studies. I am literally one of millions.

A surgeon holds a deep brain stimulation device that disrupts the brain signal symptoms of Parkinson's disease. Without animal testing the device's development would not have been possible.

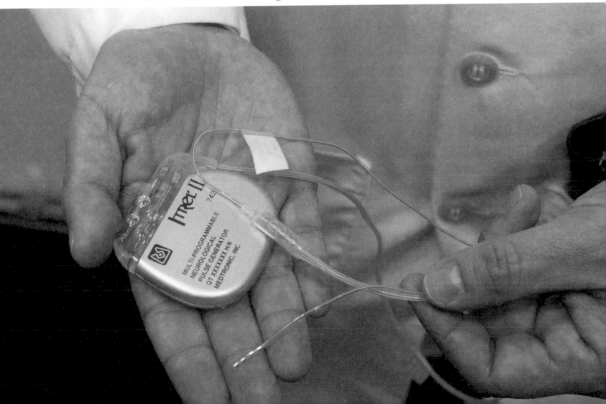

Scientists Avoid Using Animals Where They Can

In an ideal world scientists would not use animals (mainly mice and rats) for medical research. They would use alternative techniques. In fact, they are doing so increasingly. Non-animal methods now account for about 90% of medical research and include mathematical and computer models, advanced tissue and cell cultures and scanning technology.

However, the scientific consensus is that many key questions can still only be answered by animal studies. These studies offer hope to millions of people with conditions such as Alzheimer's disease, cancer, sickle cell disease, stroke, spinal cord damage and tropical diseases like malaria.

Of course, animal models have limitations. They do not always adequately mimic human disease or responses to medicines. But they remain crucial and have made a major contribution to many of the biggest medical advances of our age.

EVALUATING THE AUTHORS' ARGUMENTS:

Winston and Illman claim that some of the most important medical advances humans have ever made—such as penicillin, blood transfusion, and organ transplants—came about as the result of animal testing. In their opinion, this makes the practice moral. Do you agree? Is animal testing justified if it helps save or improve the lives of humans? Why or why not? Explain your reasoning.

It Is Never Ethical to Use Animals for Medical Testing

Alistair Currie

"Means don't justify ends, so why do we think they do when it comes to animals?"

In the following viewpoint, Alistair Currie argues it is never ethical to use animals for medical testing. He says most medical procedures and drugs that are tested on animals produce results that do not translate to human scenarios. Therefore, such techniques and drugs have to be retested on humans anyway, which he says means that animals involved in testing suffer and die for nothing. But even when animal testing does yield useful information, Currie says it is wrong to think that animal lives are worth less than human lives. In his opinion, it doesn't matter that animals are not as smart, capable, or as morally or linguistically adept as humans. He points out that human rights are extended to all human beings, even those less advanced or capable than most (people in a coma, for example, or the mentally retarded, are still extended the same human rights as the brilliant and talented). Currie argues so too should animals be regarded as weak yet worthy beings who deserve to be treated with dignity and respect. He concludes that cures and medical advances do not justify hurting and killing animals because animal lives are worth as much as human lives.

Currie is senior research and campaigns coordinator for the UK affiliate of People for the Ethical Treatment of Animals.

AS YOU READ, CONSIDER THE FOLLOWING QUESTIONS:
1. What percentage of drugs that pass animal tests fail in humans, according to Currie?
2. What does Currie say is the basis of human rights? What does he say that means for animal rights?
3. Currie implies that governments, scientists, and terrorists have what in common?

A t its heart, the case for animal experimentation rests on a simple utilitarian equation: animal suffering in medical research is worth less than the human benefit that results. This received wisdom appears rational and self-evident but the simplicity of the utilitarian argument is no more than the attractive face of an ugly reality.

Human and Animal Rights Are Linked
If utilitarianism were really our guiding principle, we would experiment on ourselves. Ninety per cent of drugs that pass animal tests fail in humans and billions of dollars are wasted on animal research that leads us down blind alleys. Involving people in the dangerous, speculative early stages of medical research would yield benefits for the rest of us. But we don't believe that sacrificing a few babies would be worth it if it helped to cure cancer—and we are absolutely right. Means don't justify ends, so why do we think they do when it comes to animals?

This discrimination relies on difference (as the abuse of the weak by the strong always does). Animals lack our mental powers, moral capacities and a place in our community, goes the argument. But we don't apply that principle to our own mentally, socially or morally subnormal and experiment on the sick, the isolated or the criminal. Universal human rights don't rest on our capacities, which are not universal, but on our vulnerabilities, which are. If we can be hurt and if we value our lives, we earn the right to moral protection. Animals suffer and want to live too. If we recognise that the basis of human rights is the protection of the weak, we cannot deny the most basic of those rights to others who suffer and are powerless.

Millions of Animals Have Died in Vain

Animals aren't means to our ends—but even if they were, the calculation is wrong. The only sure outcomes of animal experiments are dead animals. Millions of animal experiments have failed to yield cures to AIDS, strokes, Alzheimer's and other diseases. How can we say that a

PETA advocates in Britain hold a blindfold vigil to protest Oxford University's use of animals in labs.

Common Tests Performed on Animals

Toxicity tests are tests that scientists perform on animals to determine whether a substance will be harmful to humans. Many toxicity tests explore specific harmful effects, such as eye irritation or cancer, and some last for the duration of an animal's life–in some cases, their offspring are tested.

Acute systemic toxicity: Whether a chemical causes death or sickness after it is forced into an animal orally, nasally, or through its skin.

Skin irritation/corrosion: Whether a chemical causes skin damage that is either reversible or irreversible.

Eye irritation/corrosion: Whether a chemical causes eye damage that is reversible or irreversible.

Skin sensitization: Whether a chemical causes a skin allergy.

Skin absorption: How much and how quickly a chemical is able to enter the body via the skin.

Repeated dose toxicity: Whether a chemical causes general toxicological effects that occur as a result of repeated daily exposure to a substance (via oral, inhalation, and/or skin routes) for a portion of the expected life span (i.e., 1 to 3 months) or for the majority of the life span (i.e., 14 to 24 months).

Reproductive and developmental toxicity: Whether a chemical causes damage to sexual function, fertility, and/or normal offspring development (i.e., spontaneous abortion, premature delivery, and birth defects). This is determined by breeding and testing one or more generations of offspring.

Genetic toxicity: Whether a chemical causes genetic mutations and/or other alterations of genetic material.

Carcinogenicity: Whether a chemical causes cancer.

Immunotoxicity: How toxic a chemical is to a creature's immune system.

Neurotoxicity: How toxic/what effect a chemical has on the brain, spinal cord, and/or peripheral nervous system.

Taken from: Humane Society of the United States, 2009.

speculative theoretical benefit outweighs the known cost in suffering and death? This isn't balancing saving a dog against saving a duchess—it's balancing a known against an unknown. And, crucially, that's something we don't need to do.

It Is Money, Not Research, That Is Needed

According to Unicef, around 10 million children under five die of preventable causes each year. Meanwhile, if you're working class in the UK, you're likely to die seven years earlier than a professional. Forty percent of all cancers can be prevented and many can be cured yet, to quote the World Health Organisation "more than 70% of all cancer deaths occur in . . . countries, where resources available for prevention, diagnosis and treatment . . . are limited or nonexistent." If saving lives is our goal, we can achieve that without a single mouse being given cancer or a single monkey poisoned to death.

If cost-benefit is our guide, why not sell our iPods and use the money to buy life-saving mosquito nets? While those of us who are fortunate and privileged are unwilling to live a little less comfortably to save people ourselves, we earnestly endorse the wholesale killing of animals on the merest possibility of benefit. Talk of a moral obligation to inflict harm is scant: sacrificing others before making the merest sacrifice yourself is a long, long way from doing the right thing.

> # FAST FACT
>
> A common test performed on research animals is the LD50 test, or the "median lethal dose." This test determines the amount of a substance that will kill 50 percent of the animals given that dosage. The substance is given orally, topically, intravenously, or through inhalation, usually to rats, mice, rabbits, and guinea pigs. Substances tested include household products, drugs, or pesticides.

We Should Never Endorse Cruelty

We can have medical research without animals but the issue is bigger than that. The case for inflicting justified harm—whether made by governments, scientists or terrorists—must always be treated with suspicion. Animal experimentation is an act of unconscious hypocrisy by a society whose values—including the real value we put on human life—are confused and inconsistent, and whose moral capacities are far, far more rudimentary than we like to believe.

EVALUATING THE AUTHOR'S ARGUMENTS:

Currie rests his argument on the belief that human lives are not worth more than animal lives, and so killing animals to find cures for humans is unethical. What do you think? Are human lives worth more than animal lives? Why or why not?

Facts About Animal Rights

Facts About Animals Used in Medical Research

According to the organization Pro-Test, which tracks medical research in the United Kingdom, there were 3,012,032 procedures and experiments involving animals in 2006.

Of the wide variety of institutions that use animal research:
- 42 percent are universities
- 35 percent are commercial organizations
- 5 percent are government departments
- 3 percent are non-profit organizations
- 15 percent are other public bodies

Of all the animals used:
- 69 percent were mice
- 14 percent were fish, amphibians, and reptiles
- 13 percent were rats
- 3.7 percent were birds
- 1.9 percent were sheep, cows, pigs, and other large mammals
- 1.2 percent were other rodents
- 0.7 percent were rabbits, ferrets, or other small animals
- 0.27 percent were dogs and cats specially bred for research
- 0.14 percent were monkeys, such as marmosets and macaques

Facts About Zoos

According to the World Association of Zoos and Aquariums (WAZA):
- More than 600 million visitors visit zoos and aquariums each year.
- There are about thirteen hundred international zoos and aquariums registered with WAZA.
- All members of the WAZA network are obliged to comply with WAZA's Code of Ethics and Animal Welfare.

According to the organization Quantum Conservation:
- There are more than 2,800 zoos and aquariums in the world.
- Germany has 414 registered zoos, the most in any single country.
- The United States has at least 355 zoos.

- Twenty nine zoos and aquariums in the United States have more than 1 million visitors a year.
- Busch Gardens Tampa Bay has the highest attendance, with about 4.5 million visitors annually.
- The oldest running zoo in the world is the Vienna Zoo in Schonbrunn, Germany, which dates from 1752.
- The oldest running zoo in the United States is the Philadelphia Zoo, which opened on July 1, 1874.
- The Berlin Zoo, in Germany, has the largest number of species of any zoo in the world, with over fifteen hundred species.
- The Monterey Bay Aquarium has about 124,000 individual animals and the largest number of animals in any zoo in the world.

American Opinions on Animal Rights

According to a May 2008 Gallup poll:
- 64 percent of Americans strongly support or somewhat support passing strict laws concerning the treatment of farm animals.
- 33 percent somewhat oppose or strongly oppose passing strict laws concerning the treatment of farm animals.
- 38 percent of Americans strongly support or somewhat support banning sports that involve competition between animals, such as horse racing or dog racing.
- 59 percent somewhat oppose or strongly oppose banning such sports.
- 21 percent somewhat support or strongly support banning all types of hunting.
- 77 percent of Americans strongly oppose or somewhat oppose banning all types of hunting.
- 39 percent of Americans strongly support or somewhat support banning all product testing on laboratory animals
- 59 percent strongly oppose or somewhat oppose banning all product testing on laboratory animals.
- 35 percent of Americans strongly support or somewhat support banning all medical research on laboratory animals.
- 64 percent strongly oppose or somewhat oppose banning all medical research on laboratory animals.

According to a May 2009 Gallup poll:
- 57 percent of Americans think medical testing on animals is morally acceptable.

- 36 percent think medical testing on animals is morally wrong.
- 34 percent of Americans think cloning animals is morally acceptable.
- 63 percent think cloning animals is morally wrong.
- 61 percent of Americans think buying and wearing clothes made of animal fur is morally acceptable.
- 35 percent think buying and wearing fur is morally wrong.

Organizations to Contact

American Anti-Vivisection Society (AAVS)
801 Old York Rd., Suite 204
Jenkintown, PA 19046-1685
(800) 729-2287
Web site: www.aavs.org

The AAVS is an international organization that works to end vivisection (the use of animals in research, dissection, testing, and education). The group contends that vivisection harms both people and animals by wasting time, effort, and money on research of little or no benefit, while non-animal, scientific research holds great promise for both human and animal ailments.

American Association for Laboratory Animal Science
9190 Crestwyn Hills Dr.
Memphis, TN 38125
(901) 754-8620
fax: (901) 759-5849
e-mail: info@aalas.org
Web site: www.aalas.org

The American Association for Laboratory Animal Science is a professional, nonprofit association of persons and institutions concerned with the production, care, and study of animals used in biomedical research. This organization of more than eighty-nine hundred members provides a medium for the exchange of scientific information on all phases of laboratory animal care and use through its educational activities, publications, and certification program.

American Meat Institute (AMI)
1150 Connecticut Ave. NW, 12th Floor
Washington, DC 20036
(202) 587-4200
Web site: www.meatami.com

The AMI is a membership trade organization that represents the interests of the meat and poultry industries. It researches and educates in areas such as animal welfare and food safety. The AMI Web site posts news releases, fact sheets, info kits, and visual aids relating to its position.

The American Society for the Prevention of Cruelty to Animals (ASPCA)

424 E. Ninety-second St.
New York, NY 10128
(212) 876-7700
fax: (212) 348-3031
e-mail: aspca@aspca.org
Web site: http://www.aspca.org

The ASPCA promotes appreciation for the humane treatment of animals, encourages enforcement of anticruelty laws, and works for the passage of legislation that strengthens existing laws to further protect animals. In addition to books, brochures, and videos on animal issues, the ASPCA publishes *Animal Watch*, a quarterly magazine.

The American Vegan Society

56 Dinshah Lane, PO Box 369
Malaga, NJ 08328
Web site: www.americanvegan.org

The society is dedicated to advocating a purely vegan diet, one which excludes flesh, fish, fowl, dairy products, eggs, honey, animal gelatin, and all other foods of animal origin. It also prohibits the use of animal products such as leather, wool, fur, and silk. The society publishes several brochures, booklets, books on nonviolent living and ethical eating.

American Zoo and Aquarium Association (AZA)

8403 Colesville Rd., Suite 710
Silver Spring, MD 20910-3314
(301) 562-0777
Web site: www.aza.org

AZA represents over 160 zoos and aquariums in North America. The association provides information on captive breeding of endangered species, conservation education, natural history, and wildlife legislation.

Americans for Medical Progress
526 King St., Suite 201
Alexandria, VA 22314
e-mail: amp@amprogress.org
Web site: www.amprogress.org

This nonprofit organization works to raise public awareness and education regarding medical research with animals and its importance to curing today's most devastating diseases. Its Web site offers news about the use of animals in research, as well as fact sheets and handouts.

Animal Alliance of Canada
221 Broadview Ave., Suite 101
Toronto, ON, Canada M4M 2G3
(416) 462-9541
Web site: www.animalalliance.ca

The Animal Alliance of Canada is an animal rights advocacy and education group that focuses on local, regional, national, and international issues concerning the goodwill and respectful treatment of animals by humans. Animal Alliance investigates the conditions under which millions of animals suffer each day using industry contracts, unannounced visits, literature surveys, and freedom of information legislation.

Animal Legal Defense Fund (ALDF)
170 E. Cotati Ave.
Cotati, CA 94931
(707) 795-2533
e-mail: info@aldf.org
Web site: www.aldf.org

The ALDF is an association of attorneys and law students who promote animal rights and protect the lives and interests of animals through the use of their legal skills. It publishes two newsletters, *Animals' Advocate* and *Update*.

Animal Welfare Institute (AWI)
900 Pennsylvania Ave. SE
Washington, DC 20003
(202) 337-2332
Web site: www.animalwelfare.com

The Animal Welfare Institute advocates the humane treatment of laboratory animals and the development and use of non-animal testing methods as well as encourages humane science teaching and prevention of painful experiments on animals by high school students.

Born Free USA
1122 S St.
Sacramento, CA 95811
(916) 447-3085
Web site: www.bornfreeusa.org

Born Free USA is a national animal advocacy group whose mission is to end the suffering of wild animals in captivity, rescue individual animals in need, protect wildlife—including highly endangered species—in their natural habitats, and encourage compassionate conservation globally. It works to raise awareness about animals used in entertainment, captive exotic animals, and the international wildlife trade.

Farm Animal Reform Movement (FARM)
10101 Ashburton Lane
Bethesda, MD 20817
(888) FARM-USA (327-6872)
e-mail: info@farmusa.org
Web site: www.farmusa.org

FARM seeks to moderate and eliminate animal suffering and other adverse impacts of commercial animal production. It promotes the annual observance of March 20 as the "Great American Meatout," a day of meatless meals, and provides a variety of brochures and fact sheets for consumers and activists.

Foundation for Biomedical Research (FBR)
818 Connecticut Ave. NW, Suite 303

Washington, DC 20006
(202) 457-0654
fax: (202) 457-0659
e-mail: info@fbresearch.org
Web site: www.fbresearch.org

FBR provides information and educational programs about the necessary and important role of laboratory animals in biomedical research and testing. It publishes numerous booklets and videos, including a report that chronicles illegal activities undertaken by animal rights activists.

The Great Ape Project (GAP)
PO Box 19492
Portland, OR, 97280-0492
(503) 222-5755
fax: (503) 238-5884
Web site: www.greatapeproject.org

GAP, an international organization, works to include great apes within the category of persons. It advocates that due to their humanlike mental capacities and emotions, great apes deserve the same basic moral and legal rights as people enjoy. GAP publishes a free newsletter and numerous books.

Humane Society of the United States (HSUS)
2100 L St. NW
Washington, DC 20037
(202) 452-1100
Web site: www.hsus.org

HSUS encourages respect, understanding, and compassion for all creatures. Among its many diverse efforts, it maintains programs that support responsible pet ownership and the elimination of cruelty in hunting and trapping. It also exposes painful uses of animals in research and testing and abusive treatment of animals in movies, circuses, pulling contests, and racing. It campaigns for animal protection legislation and monitors the enforcement of existing animal protection statutes.

Incurably Ill for Animal Research
PO Box 27454
Lansing, MI 48909
(517) 887-1141
Web site: www.iifar.org

This organization consists of people who have incurable diseases and are concerned that the use of animals in medical research will be stopped or severely limited by animal rights activists, thus delaying or preventing the development of new cures. It publishes the monthly *Bulletin* and a quarterly newsletter.

Institute for Animal Rights Law
Post Office Box F
Clarks Summit, PA 18411
(800) 543.ISAR (-4727)
Web Site: www.instituteforanimalrightslaw.org

This organization provides legal information, analysis, and guidance for the animal rights and animal welfare movements. Among other accomplishments, it has drafted state and federal animal protection legislation, advises public officials and animal rights groups about legal rights of animals, and educates the public about animal rights issues. Its Web site offers articles pertaining to animal rights law.

Institute for In Vitro Sciences (IIVS)
30 W. Watkins Mill Rd., Suite 100
Gaithersburg, MD 20878
(301) 947-6523
Web site: www.iivs.org

IIVS is a nonprofit, technology-driven, foundation for the advancement of alternative methods to animal testing. In order to facilitate the reduction of animal use in testing, the institute promotes the optimization, use, and acceptance of in vitro methodologies worldwide. *In vitro* literally means "in glass," and refers to an artificial environment — such as a test tube — outside a living organism. IIVS makes its published articles available on its Web site.

Institute of Laboratory Animal Research (ILAR)

500 Fifth St. NW
Washington, DC 20001
(202) 334-3600
Web site: http://dels.nas.edu/ilar/

Organized under the auspices of the National Academy of Sciences, ILAR advises, upon request, the federal government and other agencies concerning the use of animals in biomedical research. It prepares guidelines and policy papers on biotechnology, the use of animals in precollege education, and other topics in laboratory animal science.

Medical Research Modernization Committee (MRMC)

3200 Morley Rd.
Shaker Heights, OH 44122
Web site: www.mrmcmed.org

The MRMC is a national health advocacy group composed of physicians, scientists, and other health care professionals who evaluate benefits, risks, and costs of medical research methods and technologies. Together they support using animals for medical research. In fact, the MRMC attributes the steadily increasing incidence of cancer, AIDS, and other uniquely human diseases to inadequate treatment approaches derived from research programs based on artificial and unnatural laboratory models.

People for the Ethical Treatment of Animals (PETA)

501 Front St.
Norfolk, VA 23510
(757) 622-PETA (-7382)
fax: (757) 622-0457
e-mail: peta@norfolk.infi.net
Web site: www.peta.org

An international animal rights organization, PETA is dedicated to establishing and protecting the rights of animals. It focuses on four areas: factory farms, research laboratories, the fur trade, and the entertainment industry. PETA promotes public education, cruelty investigations, animal rescue, celebrity involvement, and legislative and direct action. It produces numerous videos, brochures, reports, and other publications.

Physicians Committee for Responsible Medicine (PCRM)
5100 Wisconsin Ave. NW, Suite 400
Washington, DC 20016
(202) 686-2210
fax: (202) 686-2216
e-mail: pcrm@pcrm.org
Web site: www.pcrm.org

Founded in 1985, PCRM is a nonprofit organization supported by physicians and laypersons to encourage higher standards for ethics and effectiveness in research. It promotes using animal alternatives in both research and education. The committee publishes the quarterly magazine *Good Medicine* and numerous fact sheets on animal experimentation issues.

Uncaged Campaigns
5th Floor, Alliance House
9 Leopold St.
Sheffield, S1 2GY, UK
e-mail: info@uncaged.co.uk
Web site: www.uncaged.co.uk

Uncaged Campaigns works to end vivisection and to ascribe moral and legal rights to animals. It is best known for carrying out high profile campaigns that bring in-depth knowledge of the political, legal, ethical, and scientific issues relevant to animal experimentation.

World Association of Zoos and Aquariums (WAZA)
Lindenrain 3
3012 Bern
Switzerland
e-mail: secretariat@waza.org
Web site: www.waza.org

WAZA is a pro-zoo organization whose mission is to guide, encourage, and support zoos, aquariums, and like-minded organizations of the world in animal care and welfare, environmental education, and global conservation.

Zoocheck Canada
788¹/₂ O'Connor Dr.
Toronto, ON, Canada M4B 2S6
(416) 285-1744
e-mail: zoocheck@zoocheck.com
Web site: www.zoocheck.com

Zoocheck works to improve wildlife protection in Canada and to end the abuse, neglect, and exploitation of individual wild animals. The organization is a leading voice for the protection of wild animals and the only Canadian organization with a specific focus on captive wild animal issues and problems.

For Further Reading

Books

Beers, Diane L. *For the Prevention of Cruelty: The History and Legacy of Animal Rights Activism in the United States.* Cleveland: Swallow Press, 2006. Chronicles the history of the animal rights movement, suggesting that animal rights activism has been far more successful historically and has had a far greater impact on society than previously believed.

Bekoff, Marc. *The Emotional Lives of Animals: A Leading Scientist Explores Animal Joy, Sorrow, and Empathy—and Why They Matter.* Novato, CA: New World Library, 2008. A scientist explores decades of animal research to determine that animals have feelings and explains why readers should accept both the existence and significance of animal emotions.

Bronner, Simon J. *Killing Tradition: Inside Hunting and Animal Rights Controversies.* Lexington: University of Kentucky Press, 2008. Reflects on the social, psychological, and anthropological issues relating to hunting.

Carbone, Larry. *What Animals Want: Expertise and Advocacy in Laboratory Animal Welfare Policy.* New York: Oxford University Press, 2004. A laboratory veterinarian discusses the particulars of animal research.

Conn, P. Michael, and James V. Parker. *The Animal Research War.* New York: Palgrave Macmillan, 2008. Analyzes the effect of animal extremism on the world's scientists, their institutions, and professional societies.

Dawn, Karen. *Thanking the Monkey: Rethinking the Way We Treat Animals.* New York: HarperPaperbacks, 2008. An overview of the major issues in animal rights.

Greek, Jean Swingle, and C. Ray Greek. *What Will We Do If We Don't Experiment On Animals? Medical Research for the Twenty-First Century.* Bloomington, IN: Trafford Publishing, 2006. Two doctors argue that animal experiments are unnecessary and have resulted in both direct and indirect harm to humans.

Marcus, Erik. *Meat Market: Animals, Ethics, and Money.* Cupertino, CA: Brio Press, 2005. Exposes claims and counterclaims put forth by both the meat industry and animal rights activists.

Morrison, Adrian R. *An Odyssey with Animals: A Veterinarian's Reflections on the Animal Rights & Welfare Debate.* New York: Oxford University Press, 2009. A veterinarian and sleep researcher argues that humane animal use in biomedical research is an indispensable tool of medical science and that efforts to halt such use constitute a grave threat to human health and well-being.

Shevelow, Kathryn. *For the Love of Animals: The Rise of the Animal Protection Movement.* New York: Holt Paperbacks, 2009. Argues that a change in attitudes toward animals has come painfully slowly and that the fight for further protection is far from finished.

Smith, Wesley J. *A Rat Is a Pig Is a Dog Is a Boy: The Human Cost of the Animal Rights Movement.* New York: Encounter Books, 2010. Argues against animal rights rhetoric, contending that humanity has an obligation to people and offering rights to animals would threaten human dignity.

Sunstein, Cass R., and Martha C. Nussbaum, eds. *Animal Rights: Current Debates and New Directions.* New York: Oxford University Press, 2005. A collection of essays exploring the legal and political issues that underlie the campaign for animal rights and the opposition to it.

Torres, Bob. *Making A Killing: The Political Economy of Animal Rights.* Oakland, CA: AK Press, 2007. Explores the similarities shared by human and animal oppression and how both are exploited by the capitalist system.

Williams, Erin E., and Margo DeMello. *Why Animals Matter: The Case for Animal Protection.* Amherst, NY: Prometheus Books, 2007. Exposes how mass production of animals for food and other purposes results in cruelty that usually remains hidden from sight.

Periodicals

Al-Qasimi, Nouf. "The Meat (and Vegetables) of the Matter," *National,* November 3, 2009. www.thenational.ae/apps/pbcs.dll/article?AID =/20091104/LIFE/711039979/1086/magazine.

Ball, Matt, and Bruce Friedrich. "Why Progressives Should Care About Animal Rights," Alternet, June 23, 2009. www.alternet.org/environ

ment/140678/why_progressives_should_care_about_animal_rights/?
page=entire.

Cavanaugh, Tim. "The Shifting Frontiers of Animal Rights: Activists Yawn as Animals Lurch Toward a Hybrid Future," *Reason,* August–September, 2009. http://reason.com/archives/2009/07/21/the-shifting-frontiers-of-anim.

Cook, Kristina. "Pro-Test: Supporting Animal Testing," *Spiked,* February 23, 2006. www.spiked-online.com/Articles/0000000CAF94.htm.

Douglas, Kate. "Just Like Us: Humans Have Rights, Other Animals Don't—No Matter How Human-Like They Are," *New Scientist,* June 2, 2007.

Festing, Simon. "Animal Research—a Defence," *New Statesman,* March 14, 2008. www.newstatesman.com/life-and-society/2008/03/animal-research-rights-debate.

Foer, Jonathan Safran. "Eating Animals Is Making Us Sick," CNN.com, October 28, 2009. www.cnn.com/2009/OPINION/10/28/opinion.jonathan.foer/index.html.

Francione, Gary L. "One Right for All: We Treat Animals How We Used to Treat Human Slaves. What Possible Justification Is There for That?" *New Scientist,* October 8, 2005.

Geoghegan, Tom. "What Are Zoos For?" *BBC News Magazine,* January 8, 2008. http://news.bbc.co.uk/2/hi/uk_news/magazine/7175652.stm.

George, Justin. "Animal Liberation and Participatory Theory," *Z Magazine,* February 11, 2009. http://www.zmag.org/znet/viewArticlePrint/20535.

Global Agenda. "Deep-Fried Kittens; Fish; PETA's Dangerous New Campaign," January 26, 2009.

Haspal, Tamar. "Meat Eaters Without the Guilt," *Washington Post,* August 14, 2006. www.washingtonpost.com/wpdyn/content/article/2006/08/13/AR2006081300715.html.

Kuipers, Dean, interviewed by Vanessa Kerr. "Terrorism Laws Are Wrongly Being Used to Round Up Eco-Activists, Says Author Dean Kuipers," *Grist,* July 23, 2009. www.grist.org/article/2009-07-23-terrorism-laws-used-to-round-up-eco-activists-dean-kuipers.

McArdle, Megan. "Why I Eat Meat," *Atlantic,* December 14, 2007. http://meganmcardle.theatlantic.com/archives/2007/12/why_i_eat_meat.php.

Meeropal, Rachel. "The Animal Enterprise Terrorism Act: The Most Dangerous Domestic Terror Law You've Never Heard Of," Alternet, July 15, 2009. www.alternet.org/rights/141328/the_animal_enter prise_terrorism_act:_the_most_dangerous_domestic_terror_law_ you've_never_heard_of/.

Miller, John J. "In the Name of the Animals: America Faces a New Kind of Terrorism," *National Review,* July 3, 2006.

New York Times. "Primates Aren't Pets," February 25, 2009. www.nytimes.com/2009/02/25/opinion/25wed4.html.

New York Times. "When Human Rights Extend to Nonhumans," 2007. www.nytimes.com/2008/07/13/weekinreview/13mcneil .html?pagewanted=2&_r=2&ref=science.

Nickerson, Colin. "Are the Lab Rat's Days Numbered?" *Boston Globe,* March 30, 2009. www.boston.com/business/healthcare/articles/ 2009/03/30/are_the_lab_rats_days_numbered/.

O'Neill, Terry. "Animal Rights and the Culture of Death," *Catholic Insight,* November 2008.

Pickert, Kate. "Undercover Animal Rights Investigator," *Time,* March 9, 2009. www.time.com/time/nation/article/0,8599,1883742,00.html.

Planck, Nina. "Death by Veganism," *New York Times,* May 21, 2007. www.nytimes.com/2007/05/21/opinion/21planck.html?ex=133740 0000&en=37878847a13bd4bc&ei=5090.

Portman, Natalie. "Jonathan Safran Foer's *Eating Animals* Turned Me Vegan," *HuffingtonPost,* October 27, 2009. www.huffingtonpost .com/natalie-portman/jonathan-safran-foers-iea_b_334407.html.

Reed, Barney. "An Issue That Polarises," *New Statesman,* February 28, 2008. www.newstatesman.com/society/2008/02/animal-suffering-rights-rspca.

Roche, Ansley. "Teaching Children Not to Eat Meat: Healthy or Un-ethical?" Healthy Living NYC, February 24, 2005. www.healthy livingnyc.com/article/117.

Smith, Wesley J. "Monkey Business," *Weekly Standard,* July 21, 2008. www.weeklystandard.com/Content/Public/Articles/000/000/015/32 1itvqn.asp?pg=1.

Smith, Wesley J. "Veganism Is Murder," *National Review,* July 22, 2008. http://article.nationalreview.com/?q=MTM5YTMxZTVh NjllNTM4OWE4NTdhYmJmM2EwNWZiNzI.

Smith, Wesley J. "Why We Call Them Human Rights," *Weekly Standard,* November 24, 2008. www.weeklystandard.com/Content/Pub lic/Articles/000/000/015/823qaarg.asp?pg=1.

Somerville, Margaret. "Dolphins and Chimpanzees Should Be Respected, but They Are Not Persons," MercatorNet, January 27, 2010. www.mercatornet.com/articles/view/are_animals_persons.

Steiner, Gary. "Animal, Vegetable, Miserable," *New York Times,* November 21, 2009. www.nytimes.com/2009/11/22/opinion/22steiner .html?pagewanted=1&_r=1.

Stossel, John. "Eat the Tigers!" Townhall.com, May 13, 2009. http://townhall.com/columnists/JohnStossel/2009/05/13/eat_the_ti gers!?page=full&comments=true.

Wolff, Jonathan, and Kenneth Boyd. "Animal Rights and Wrongs: Campaigners Who Stand Up for Animal Research Should Be Careful Not to Oversimplify the Debate," *New Scientist,* March 11, 2006.

Young, Barbara. "Battling Anti-Meat Terrorists," *National Provisioner,* December 2008.

Web Sites

Animal Concerns Community (www.animalconcerns.org). The Animal Concerns Community is a project of the EnviroLink Network, a non-profit organization which has been providing access to thousands of online environmental and animal rights/welfare resources since 1991. The community serves as a clearinghouse for information on the Internet related to animal rights and welfare.

Animal Freedom.org (www.animalfreedom.org). This Web site serves as a virtual community for animal rights activists worldwide to exchange ideas about how to end factory farming and promote animals rights.

Animal Rights.net (www.animalrights.net). This anti–animal rights Web site offers breaking news stories about animal rights activists who break the law or otherwise cross a line for the sake of animal rights.

Animal Rights: The Abolitionist Approach (www.abolitionist approach.com). This site seeks to promote a variation of animal rights that promotes the complete abolition of animal exploitation and regards veganism as the moral baseline of the animal rights position. It advocates that no animal products, such as leather or honey, be used by humans.

Animal Rights History (www.animalrightshistory.org/). This Web site provides historical literature on animal rights and animal welfare.

Animal Scam (www.animalscam.com). This site provides information and news about animal rights activists, arguing they are hysterical and overly panicked about the status of animals.

National Anti-Vivisection Society: Who Tests on Animals (http://www.navs.org/site/PageServer?pagename=ain_pt_whois). This site allows users to type in names of their favorite products and companies to determine whether or not they engage in animal testing.

Pro-Test (www.pro-test.org.uk). This site campaigns in favor of continued animal testing and in support of scientific research. Information on the site aims to dispel myths promoted by anti-vivisectionists and to encourage people to stand up for science and human progress.

Index

Veganism
  is unhealthy, 84–90
  as only ethical diet, 78–83
Vegetarianism, 66, 71–72, 74, 78–79
Vick, Michael, 81

Vitamin D, 87

W
Watson, David, 83
Wilberforce, William, 41
Wise, Stephen, 27